STAND UP
FOR YOURSELF!

'Most people who sexually abuse teenagers and children expect you to stand there and take it. And most of the time, that's exactly what happens. You can change that.

Learn how to be safe outside, at home, at school, and anywhere else you might be. This means not only knowing how to recognise the people, places and situations that might be dangerous, but also knowing how to act like somebody no one would mess around with.'

Helen Benedict

The author gratefully acknowledges permission to reprint excerpts from:

Adolescent Sexuality in Contemporary America by Robert C. Sorenson. Copyright © 1972, 1973, Robert C. Sorenson. Reprinted by permission of Harry N. Abrams, Inc.

The Silent Children by Linda T. Sanford. Copyright © 1980 Linda Tschirhart Sanford. Reprinted by permission of Doubleday and Company, Inc.

Men Who Rape, by A. Nicholas Groth with H. Jean Birnbaum. Copyright © 1979 Plenum Press. Reprinted by permission.

Text copyright © 1987 Helen Benedict

First published in 1987 as *Safe, Strong and Streetwise*,
by Little, Brown and Company, USA

First published in Great Britain 1988
by Hodder and Stoughton Children's Books
and simultaneously by Lightning

This edition published by
Hodder Children's Books 1996

Revised and updated by Rachel Bladon

Illustrations copyright © 1996 Lauren Child

The right of Helen Benedict and Lauren Child to be identified as
the author and illustrator of the work has been asserted by them
in accordance with the Copyright, Designs and Patents Act 1988

Designed by Claire S. Bicknell
Cover design by Vic Groombridge

10 9 8 7 6 5 4 3 2 1

ISBN 0340 65587 9

A Catalogue record for this book is available
from the British Library.

Hodder Children's Books
A division of Hodder Headline plc
338 Euston Road
London NW1 3BH

Printed and bound by Cox & Wyman Ltd, Reading, Berks

STAND UP FOR YOURSELF!

Helen Benedict

illustrations by Lauren Child

h

*Hodder
Children's
Books*

a division of Hodder Headline plc

To my son, Simon

Acknowledgments

Thank you to all the teenagers who spoke to me for this book, and to all the adults who recalled past experiences they allowed me to use. Thanks also to Michael Castleman, A.Nicholas Groth, Linda Sanford, Robert Sorensen, Flora Colao, and Tamar Hosansky for the information in their valuable books. Finally, thanks to my husband, Stephen O'Connor, for his patient readings, and to Jenny Roberts for her careful editing and research.

Contents

Contents

INTRODUCTION

As a teenager, you are changing from a child to a sexual being. You are on the threshold of the biggest change in your life, for not only do you feel different when you become a sexual being, you are seen as different by the rest of the world.

Becoming a sexual being brings up all kinds of issues - some wonderful, some difficult - and you have a right to know all you can about how to handle your new status. Knowing about the dangers of sex as well as its pleasures will help you develop a happy, healthy and safe sexual life. It will protect you not only from the misunderstandings that can lead a boyfriend, girlfriend or acquaintance to hurt you, but from the harm anyone might intentionally want to do to you.

The most common types of sexual abuse happen almost every day, especially to girls: being jeered at in the street, being touched in a sexual way against your will, seeing a flasher, being touched up by a stranger, being pushed to go too far by a boyfriend or girlfriend.

The next most common type of abuse happens when an adult or older teenager, usually someone you know, tries to use your body in a sexual way that you don't like.

Finally, there is the more remote chance that you might be seriously sexually assaulted or raped.

This book will address all the kinds of sexual abuse you might come across, from the most mild to the most serious. It will show you how best to protect yourself from strangers, how to recognise and avoid sexual assault by people you know, and how to handle everyday abuse.

Adult men and teenage boys can also be rape victims, and statistics show that young boys are abused almost as often as girls. On a recent live video show a man phoned in to tell me,

I was raped when I was ten by my uncle. I kept it a secret for twenty years. I never dared tell anyone about it because no one

ever talked about male assault in those days. I lived a life of self-destruction and drugs, always looking for other people who'd been hurt as much as I was.

I hope that this book will not only make you safer, but will help you feel stronger and braver. Just because you want to protect yourself, it doesn't mean you can't enjoy yourself. Hopefully, most of you will never have to confront the more serious kinds of abuse dealt with in this book. But the more you learn about how to protect yourself and about your sexual rights, the less helpless you'll feel. And not feeling helpless means being able to enjoy life – and love – a great deal more.

WHY YOU NEED THIS BOOK

Most of us think defensively whenever the subject of sexual assault comes up. 'If I'm just a little sensible,' we tell ourselves, 'I won't have to worry about all the perverts out there looking for victims.'

If only that were true. Unfortunately, being 'just a little sensible' doesn't always help. We are tempted to believe that only people who are delinquent or careless get assaulted, because that makes us feel immune, but the truth is that assailants rarely care who we are, what we are like, or how we feel. Their only concern is that we are available for attack.

In the crime of sexual assault, the selection of victims is particularly random. A burglar may prefer to rob people who are rich, or who live in a neighbourhood he knows, but a rapist only cares about how easily he can get at us. That's why trying to define a typical victim is always so difficult. A victim of sexual assault can be anyone from a two-month-old baby to a woman in her nineties. We can be assaulted whether we are poor or rich, thin or fat, black or white. We can be assaulted regardless of our sex, personality, religion, nationality, background, education, or class. Every one of us is vulnerable to sexual abuse.

What is sexual abuse?

Sexual abuse is a general term which means the use of sex in a harmful or unwanted way. Some types of sexual abuse are criminal offences, which means that the person who commits them can be taken to court and prosecuted. These offences are classed as sexual assault. It is important to understand the different types of sexual assault so that you know if you are being assaulted and so you can decide what to do about it.

Rape This happens when a boy or man has sexual intercourse with a girl against her will. That means he puts his penis in her vagina by using threats, force or deception. He may threaten to kill the victim; he may beat the victim up or simply use brute force; or he may trick the victim by making threats and promises.

Indecent assault This means forcing sexual contact on someone. For instance, your boyfriend forces you to go further than you want; your father fondles your genitals; a stranger touches your buttocks or breasts. The most extreme cases of indecent assault can be classed as attempted rape.

Indecent Exposure This is when a man exposes his penis to a female in an obscene and insulting way in public.

Buggery This means anal intercourse. It is illegal unless both partners are over 18 and consenting.

If you are a boy, you can be assaulted in the same way as a girl. You can be abused by men, women or other boys.

Some sexual abuses are so subtle that they are hard to recognise. Sometimes it's hard to know whether you are really being forced to do things, and therefore whether you have a right to complain. The best way to clarify any confusion is to examine exactly how you feel about the act you are being asked to do. If you feel dread, fear or shock, horror, humiliation, disgust, or even just reluctance, you are being abused.

Why does sexual abuse hurt?

Rapists, molesters, incestuous parents, and other sexual offenders always try to justify their behaviour so that it doesn't seem criminal or cruel. They argue that they haven't hurt their victims. This is simply not true. All sexual abuses hurt, physically and emotionally. No one ever wants to be forced into a sexual act.

Whether you are male or female, eleven or twenty, you want to choose when and how to have sexual encounters. Your first dignity is your right over your own body.

When someone abuses you sexually, he takes that dignity away. He ignores your feelings and your personality. He hurts you, degrades you, makes you feel small and worthless and full of guilt, and then tries to tell you that you liked it.

Many victims are deeply traumatised because they thought they were going to be mutilated or murdered. Seventeen-year-old Karen was raped by a man she'd just met in a park.

When I was raped, I thought I was going to die. I thought the guy was going to kill me. I remember I begged and cried for him not to kill me; that's probably just what he wanted. He dragged me behind some bushes and waved a lead pipe at me and told me to take my clothes off. Then he pushed me on the ground where it was cold and dirty and lay on top of me and had sex with me. He hit me a lot to keep me quiet. I was in pain all over, but none of it was as bad as the fear that he would kill me.

This thirteen-year-old boy was assaulted by his babysitter:

I was about thirteen and she was eighteen or nineteen. She was babysitting for me. I came into the kitchen, and she dragged me into the bedroom. I

13

didn't know what was happening. She pulled down my pants and masturbated me. Then she lay down on the bed and put me on top of her. It was painful. Her pubic hair was sharp, and it felt like spikes were cutting and sticking me. I was shaking and trembling. It scared the hell out of me. I didn't tell anybody about it, but after that, I told my mother I didn't want a babysitter any more, and I stayed by myself.

Physically, sexual assault can be extremely painful. There is a common myth that rape doesn't actually hurt victims, it just frightens them, but that is not true. Forced sexual intercourse in any circumstance hurts a lot. Some victims say it felt like their skin was being torn apart. Molestation can hurt physically, too, especially if violence is used, for the genital area is tender and vulnerable.

However old you are, sex should never make you feel all these negative things. It should make you feel happy and relaxed. Above all, it should make you feel loved. Sex that makes you feel unhappy should never happen. Now you can learn to prevent it.

What you already know

We all know something about how to protect ourselves. Your earliest memories may include being taught not to get into a car with strangers, for instance. You probably also know that you shouldn't walk down dark alleyways at night, or hang around in certain parts of town. But many of us ignore what we already know. And many of us think we know more about self-protection than we really do. Listen to these teenagers, all of whom live in a big city and consider themselves streetwise:

◆ *I stay in my neighbourhood, where it's safe.*

◆ *I don't walk around alone at night.*

◆ *I walk with friends after dark.*

◆ *I ring my mother and tell her where I'm going.*

All these precautions are sensible, but they are not enough. It is a good idea to stay in a neighbourhood you know well, but that doesn't mean you are safe: many rapes take place in or around the victim's home. In fact, you should be more cautious near your home, not less. It is also wise to avoid being alone when out at night, in order to protect yourself against strangers, but that is only half the battle: many rape victims know their attackers. And letting your mother know where you are is always a good idea, but if you are somewhere unsafe, her knowledge of that might not be able to help you.

The reason most people don't know enough about how to protect themselves is simply that they were never taught. In general, a lot of adults don't teach children or teenagers self-protection because they believe that children should be allowed to be children, to be kept innocent. Unfortunately, innocent can also mean defenceless. Stereotypes about what children ought to be like should never get in the way of learning to be safe. You can learn to protect yourself without losing your idealism, your freedom or your enjoyment of life.

What can you do about sexual abuse?

Because you are young, you already have an advantage over
many would-be offenders: surprise. One of the main reasons
offenders pick on children and teenagers is because they
don't expect any resistance; they see you as an easy target. If
you know how to outwit an assailant, how to escape, and
how to defend yourself, you may be able to catch your
attacker off guard and get away.

*I was on a crowded bus coming home from school and a man
behind me started putting his hand up my shirt. So I yelled,
'This man is bothering me!' and chopped his arm away with
my hand. He moved away pretty fast. I suppose he expected
me to just stand there quietly and take it.*

Most people who sexually abuse teenagers and children *do*
expect you to stand there and take it. And most of the time,
that's exactly what happens. You can change that.

The first way to protect yourself from sexual assault is to learn
what it is, why it happens, and how often it happens; in
other words, learn to recognise the real dangers and how
vulnerable you are to them.

Then you need to learn what your sexual rights are and how to
stand up for them. This helps you avoid falling victim to
threats or your own insecurity.

Next, you have to learn how to be safe outside, at home, at
school, and anywhere else you might be. This means not only
knowing how to recognise the people, places, and situations
that might be dangerous, but also knowing how to act like
somebody no one would mess around with.

Last, but not least, you need to learn actual self-defence. This
means learning how to escape from danger before anything
happens, as well as learning how to actually fight back if you
have to.

Protecting yourself without getting paranoid

Learning to protect yourself against crime can make you feel paranoid for a while, especially at first. Many adults and children taking self-defence classes report feeling more scared than ever for the first week or two. But that soon passes. Protecting your sexual rights doesn't mean never having fun, never relaxing, or never forgetting that crime happens and might happen to you. Self-protection teaches you to exercise better judgment so that, once it has become natural to you, you feel stronger and freer than ever. Elly, who is eleven, found this out after taking a self-defence course.

Before I took the class, I was once in a cinema with a friend when a man next to me put his arm on my leg and pulled up my skirt. I hit his arm but he didn't stop. I was so scared I froze. If I'd taken self-defence then, I'd have known to yell and get attention, or to run off. Now I have taken the class, I don't feel so scared. I feel I know what to do now.

In order to protect yourself, you have to understand who offenders are and what motivates them. Understanding them helps you to avoid them.

The types of people who might sexually abuse you fall into these major categories:

◆ *Rapists or would-be rapists who assault whomever they can, regardless of the victim's age. Some of these offenders assault one sex only, some both.*

◆ *Child molesters.*

◆ *Men and women who abuse only members of their own family.*

◆ *Boys who assault their girlfriends or dates.*

Some of these offenders are your age, some are older. Some seem respectable, some are already criminals. Some may even have authority over you. The one thing they all have in common is that they don't see you as a person with your own likes, dislikes and rights. They see you as an object to use the way they want.

WHO WOULD HURT YOU
AND WHY?

Why Does Sexual Abuse Happen?

Sexual abuse never happens because of what the victim said or
did. Usually, the victim wasn't even taking a risk; they were
just going about their normal business. But even if they did
take a risk – they walked home late alone, they didn't look
behind them when they opened their door – the abuse is not

their fault. Nor is it their fault if they broke a rule or acted foolishly. When we take a risk, we do it in the hope that we won't get hurt, not that we will. When we do something careless, we are merely forgetting to consider our safety. And even when we do something 'bad', we usually assume we can get away with it. None of these acts mean we are asking to be hurt. People often try to blame sexual abuse on the victim by saying things like, 'It happened to her because she took a stupid risk,' or 'He was asking for it because he hangs out with a bad crowd.' Blaming the victim for the abuse only adds insult to injury.

Sexual abuse is caused by only one person: the offender. Why he or she does it is complicated, and some of those reasons will be dealt with in this book. One of the most basic causes of abuse, however, is the image of women in our society. From films to record covers, women and girls are depicted as sexual objects, as inferior to men, and as people to be used, not respected. A teenage girl poses like a stripper to sell jeans. A half-dressed woman is used to sell cars or whiskey. Most of the women on record covers are shown with their mouths in sexy pouts and almost nothing on. The songs themselves are full of lyrics like 'You belong to me'. 'I'm gonna get her'. Sophisticated advertisements suggest that the sign of a successful man is having a fancy car, a diamond tie pin, and a pretty woman - all possessions to show off. Women on TV advertisements either slink around in skin-tight clothes or sit at home babbling about laundry detergents. Pop videos depict women being chased, seduced, manipulated, tied up, and trodden on. Meanwhile, men and boys are presented as playing football, riding horses, making money, and getting women. The idea of women as things to get and men as the ones to get them is so pervasive in all the media that it's hard to think of an exception.

If you are a girl, these stereotyped images teach you that you are worth little unless you are beautiful and sexy, that you have no rights over your own body, and that your highest goal in life should be to catch a man and do his laundry. If you are a boy, the same images teach you that you should chase girls and catch them like rabbits, that girls don't mean it when they say no to sex, and that they're good for nothing but bed and housework. The more we are all bombarded with these images, the more we get the message that women are less than human. With that attitude, sexual abuse is easy for men to commit, and hard for women to object to.

On a more individual level, people sometimes sexually abuse others because they were sexually abused as children. The psychological explanation for this is complex, but it has a lot to do with needing to retrieve the sense of power that the assault took away. When people are sexually abused, their will and sense of control over themselves is stolen. Sometimes the only way they feel they can get it back is to repeat what was done to them on another person – usually a person the same age as they were when they were abused, this time making themselves the attacker instead of the victim.

Other offenders have learned their behaviour from watching their mothers being abused. They learn to associate violence with sex until the only kind of sex they can enjoy is sex that hurts someone. Many sexual offenders were so badly abused physically or emotionally as children that they never learned how to respect or love other people. Stopping sexual abuse is therefore essential not only to protect young people, but to prevent them from growing up to become offenders themselves.

Here is a list of the types of sexual abuse you might experience, and some other reasons why people commit them.

Street Harassment

Almost every girl and woman in this society has been yelled or whistled at in the street by a man. It happens to boys sometimes, too, but mostly it's a phenomenon directed by men at women.

Harassing women and girls in this way is such popular entertainment that there probably aren't many boys reading this book who haven't either seen friends do it, or done it themselves. 'Why not?' you might say. 'It's only in fun.'

Shouting at girls is, in fact, an act of hostility. No one shouts sexual remarks at someone he or she loves or respects. Men and boys who do shout at women do it because they think that treating women as objects is 'cool', and that it gives them the upper hand.

Harassing women and girls on the street is not only an immature way of showing off; it's a way men and boys can vent their hostility towards women without risking their own safety. Often, this hostility stems from feelings of fear or confusion about women. Some men say they resent women just because they are attracted to them: they resent the power women have over them in being desirable. Sometimes a man will harass a woman as an expression of his own insecurity – dislike for himself, perhaps, and an inability to believe that any female could really like him. Other times the hostility is based on race or class: some workmen, for example, seem to enjoy harassing women dressed in office clothing. The hostility can be disguised as flattery, but often it's right out there in the open, as Hannah found out when she was fourteen:

It was a school day at lunchtime, and I was walking to the corner to buy some yoghurt. I had to walk past a bunch of workmen, who were all sitting on the pavement eating their lunch. I felt nervous as soon as I saw them, but I didn't want to look stupid and cross the street. One of them shouted, 'Look at that ugly chick,' and then he lay down on the pavement and

*rolled over to lie at my feet. He was looking up my skirt
and laughing. I wanted to kick him in the head, but I
was too scared and humiliated. For days after that, I
hated myself for not having kicked him.*

Flashing

Young people, especially girls, are often the target of
exhibitionism, or flashing – when a man exposes his genitals
or masturbates in public.

Exhibitionists do this on buses, trains, in parks and on street
corners – wherever they can get away with it. Psychologists
say that flashers get their pleasure from the look of horror on
the victim's face, by imagining that their victim is interested
in or impressed by their genitals, or by pretending that they
are educating a young victim. Some even fantasise that they
are having a sexual relationship with their victim, or that they
are raping them. Contrary to popular belief, exhibitionists are
hardly ever senile old men in raincoats – they can be young
boys, as well as adults of all ages and types.

Molesting

Child molesters don't restrict themselves to children under
twelve, as many believe. Some pick exclusively on young
teenagers. The word 'molester' is used rather than 'rapist'
because this type of offender usually stops short of forcing
actual sexual intercourse. A few molesters aren't content with
forcing some type of sexual behaviour on their victims,
however; they want to hurt and maybe even kill. Luckily, this
last type of offender seems to be quite rare.

Molesters don't attack young people out of sexual frustration –
many of them have wives or girlfriends. Nor are they usually

gay men, as is commonly thought. Most are heterosexual or bisexual in their adult preferences. Molesters attack kids because they are thrilled by the chance to have someone helplessly in their power. For them, dominating a child has a sexual thrill.

One type of molester is known as a paedophile (peed-o-file). This person, usually male, is obsessively attracted to children. Paedophiles usually only like children of a specific age. Some only pick on one sex, others will molest both.

Paedophiles often initiate their 'relationships' by befriending their victim. They spot someone who looks lonely, neglected, or friendless and start being nice to them; they take them to places, give them presents, talk and listen to them, spend time with them. Then, gradually, they begin to make sexual advances. If the paedophile has chosen their victim well - a child who quickly becomes dependent on them for money, food, drugs, or love - they know the child won't refuse sex. A paedophile often persuades themself and their victim that they love him or her, but as soon as the victim gets too old for their taste, the paedophile loses interest. One convicted paedophile once said that the best way parents can protect their children from being sexually molested is to love them.

If the child tries to resist, the paedophile might say something like:

◆ *If you tell on me, I'll go to jail.*
  Do you want to do that to a friend?
◆ *If you tell on me, no one will believe you.*
◆ *If you tell your mother about us, the shock will*
  kill her.
◆ *If you tell on me, we'll both get into trouble.*

Paedophiles are frequently young to middle-aged men who appear outwardly normal. Contrary to popular belief, they are not necessarily retarded, insane, senile, or addicted to drink or drugs. Psychologists say that paedophiles have, in a way, never grown up. They cannot get along well with adults and only feel at ease with younger people who don't threaten or compete with them. Some paedophiles don't or can't have sexual relations with adults at all. Children make paedophiles feel young again, yet big and powerful at the same time.

Also, children are easy to intimidate into not resisting or reporting the molestation; the paedophile is very wary of getting caught.

Another type of child molester does have regular sexual relations with adults but still assaults children. He might do it to get back at somebody or some situation he is angry about. He might do it to make himself feel strong and powerful, and he may be violent with his victims. He might do it because he gets a kick out of hurting or dominating someone, and children are easier to dominate and entrap than adults. As a twenty-nine-year old man said about his attack on a boy of twelve: 'There was less trouble getting hold of kids. Kids were around and they were easy to get to, and there was less risk of getting hurt myself.'

Most molesters know the children they assault. Some – and this is true of female as well as male molesters – only assault children within their own families. Some assault their nieces, nephews, cousins or grandchildren. Others seek out work with young people in order to gain access to them.

For several reasons, molesters will try to get to know you before they assault you. They can win your trust so that you won't tell on them; they can gain the trust of your parents or guardians so that no one would believe you if you told what they did; and, most of all, they can establish power and authority over you so that it's more difficult for you to say no.

Most molesters tend to plan out their attacks, and to pick victims with care in order to protect themselves from being caught. Look at how carefully this twenty-eight-year-old offender approached his victims: 'I got busted for molesting these boys on my football team. But it wasn't like I was exploiting them. I'd worked with those kids for a full year… before I ever molested them. It took me that long before they trusted me and stopped treating me like a tough adult coach.'

It's important to remember that often, molesters don't think what they are doing is wrong. They sometimes pretend that their victims are older psychologically than they really are and that the child wanted the 'relationship' and even initiated it. In fact, what usually happens is that the victim is either so desperate for attention or love, or so frightened and bewildered, that he or she can't say no.

Rape

Rapists are men who like to humiliate and terrify people in the worst possible way: to force sex on them and to threaten them with mutilation or murder if they don't comply.

Some rapists attack out of anger. They pick the nearest convenient victim and rape that person as a kind of punishment, a revenge for whatever they are angry about. Some rapists do it to feel powerful; they want to force someone to do what they say because they find the victim's fear and submission sexually thrilling. Some believe rape is the only way they'll ever have sex because they don't think a woman would ever find them attractive. Others cannot enjoy sex unless it is violent. A few are genuine sadists and are turned on by torturing their victims. A lot of rapists are a mixture of these types. What all these men have in common is the inability to see or care about how the victim feels.

A rapist can be a fourteen-year-old boy or a forty-seven-year-old man. He can be a burglar who crawled through your window. He can be a mugger or your local policeman. He can be your boyfriend. He can be your best friend's father – or even your own.

Why a Parent Might Assault You

When a parent, a step-parent, or any other member of your family sexually assaults you, it's called incest.

Incest can be committed by siblings or mothers, but one of the most common forms is between father and daughter. The reasons why a father assaults his daughter are often the same as those described for all molesters, but there are some differences. For instance, some fathers do it because they believe a daughter is her father's property, and he has a right to do whatever he wants with her body. Some fathers go so far as to think it's their job to introduce their daughters to sex. Other fathers believe they've fallen in love with their daughters, and try to make them into substitute wives. None of these fathers recognises that their daughters are independent human beings, not possessions, and that every girl has a right to choose her own sexual partner, a right to wait until she's ready before she starts sex, and a right to look for her partner outside her home.

Parents sometimes sexually assault their sons. Occasionally, this is done for revenge. One father who assaulted his twelve-year-old son said he did it to make his wife stay home from work. A mother who sexually assaulted her sons did so because they were the only males she could have power over - adult men always beat her up. Some parents do it because their parents did it to them. The reasons and excuses are many, but none of them justify the devastating effect incest can have on the victim.

The factor that distinguishes parental incest from other sexual assaults, and that makes it especially traumatic for the victim, is that you have been forced into sex by someone on whom you are dependent for care and a home, who has legal authority over you, and whom you probably even love.

When a parent engages you in any kind of sexual activity, he or she is betraying the basic role of parents: to protect you. It is biologically and emotionally unnatural to have sex with one's own child. It is also an infringement on your rights as a human being and on your chances of happiness. What is more, it's illegal. In chapter eight you can find some advice on how to cope if you are a victim of incest.

Why Boys Date-Rape

Many girls have found themselves being forced into some kind of sexual activity by a boyfriend, or a boy they have just met.

I went to a party with a blind date arranged by a friend. When it was over, my date offered to drive me home. We started going in the wrong direction, so I asked him what he was doing. He said he was taking me back to a friend's place to hear some music. When we got there, no one was home. He jumped on me and began kissing me and fooling around. I tried to leave, but he locked the door.

We were in a part of town I didn't know. I didn't know how to get home, and it was late. It was clear that he wasn't going to let me go, and I was scared of him. So I said, 'OK, let's just do it.' I couldn't even speak I was so angry - with him, with myself, even with the whole situation. I felt awful.

Sexual assault by a boy you know can take many forms, from the obvious rape described above, committed with threats and physical force, to a kind that's so subtle you're not sure whether it's force or seduction. The boy might suddenly jump on you the minute you are alone, like the boy did above, or he might try some of these kinds of threats:

◆ *If you don't do it, I'll tell everyone you did anyway.*

◆ *If you don't do it, I'll leave you.*

◆ *He might try to force you with insults, or he might try to pressurise you with emotional blackmail:*

◆ *If you love me, you'll do it.*

◆ *Don't you like me or something?*

◆ *If you refuse me, I'll hurt myself.*

Or, he might simply refuse to take no for an answer.

Whether the boy is trying to pressurise you to have sexual intercourse or to just make you touch his body or let him touch yours, as long as it's against your will, it's sexual abuse. It can happen at a party, in your house when your parents are out, at school - wherever he can get you alone. What is more, the boy will probably think he hasn't done anything wrong.

There are a lot of destructive myths in our society that actually encourage boys to force girls into sexual acts. One myth is that girls never like sex, so they have to be pushed into it. Another myth is that a girl owes a boy sex if he takes her out, spends money on her, or fondles and kisses her. An especially widespread myth is that girls always say no to sex but never mean it. If a boy is heavily exposed to these sorts of myths without correction, he may learn to be so selfish about sex that he thinks only about what he wants, not what the girl wants. He may come to believe, like this young man quoted below – who raped and seriously beat a woman on their second date – that he has a right to 'take' a woman's body whenever he wants to. 'I think I was really pissed off at her because it didn't go as planned. I could have been with someone else. She led me on but wouldn't deliver... I have a male ego that must be fed.'

Why Boys Gang Rape

Most group rapes are committed by teenage boys. They usually attack a girl their own age, but occasionally they assault a boy. They do it to show off to each other, to follow the crowd, to make themselves look tough and dangerous, and because, like all sexual offenders, they don't see their victims as human. Usually a gang rape is instigated by the leader of the group, and the others follow because they are afraid to look chicken or unmasculine.

3

YOUR SEXUAL RIGHTS
AND RESPONSIBILITIES

The essence of knowing how to protect yourself is knowing the
rights and responsibilities that go along with being a sexual
person. You need to know your sexual rights because this will
help you to recognise, prevent and avoid all kinds of sexual
assault. You need to know your sexual responsibilities so that
you can avoid hurting other people. Most important of all,
knowing your sexual rights and responsibilities helps you
enjoy sex in the best way possible.

Your Sexual Rights

1. *You have a right to enjoy sex.*

    When there's a lot of talk about sexual abuse, it's sometimes
    hard to remember that sex itself is a beautiful, natural
    experience – or it should be.

2.   *You have a right to wait until you're ready for sex.*

One of the main ways to guarantee that you will enjoy sex is to wait until you're ready. Don't make yourself start sex before you really want to just to please a partner or keep up with the crowd. Here is the testimony of a fourteen-year-old girl who let this happen to her:

I forced myself not to feel bad when they touched me, because I feared I was frigid or weird or something like that. So I gritted my teeth. I didn't dislike what they were doing, but it was the way they made me feel while they were doing it. That's what made me stop.

If the idea of sex frightens or disgusts you, you aren't ready yet and you aren't going to be able to enjoy it. No one has the right to pressurise you into doing something which you find unappealing.

The main reason people make love before they are ready is because they think their partner expects it. Misunderstandings like this happen between couples because of myths about the way males and females behave. Boys, it is believed, always want sex no matter what: they're always ready for it. Because of this myth, boys often think they've got to initiate sex and follow it through whenever they have the chance, even if they don't feel like it. And girls think they'd better please the boy or else they'll be torturing him.

Girls, on the other hand, are thought either never to want sex or always to pretend they don't want it. This myth makes boys think they have to pressurise the girl, and that when she says no, she's only acting.

The truth is that boys, as much as girls, can be scared by sex. They might be afraid because they don't think they're very good at it yet, and they fear the girl will laugh at them. They might not feel emotionally ready for sex yet, or not be attracted enough to the girl. Or they might be afraid that something will go wrong, like not getting an erection, ejaculating too early, or not satisfying the girl. If you, as a boy, don't feel like having sex, don't scold yourself for being abnormal – you're not.

The truth about girls is that they do, of course, like making love, but often not until they are somewhat older than the age at which boys are ready. Also, girls usually prefer to trust and like the boy they make love with. When a girl says yes, she means it; when she says no, she means that, too.

Everyone has a healthier sex life if they don't push themselves too soon.

3. You always have a right to say no.

Susie's father said to her, 'I made you, so you belong to me. You have to do what I want.' He forced sex on her from age ten to thirteen and she thought she had no right to say no.

If a person with authority over you, like a teacher or a parent, tries to order you to have sex, you have an absolute right to refuse. You don't belong to anyone else – not a parent, not a boyfriend or girlfriend, not any authority figure, not anyone who loves you, not anyone you love.

If a boyfriend tries to pressurise you to have sex against your will in the name of 'love', you also have a right to say no.

Your right to say no never changes, no matter what the circumstances. If you've broken a rule, like going out with a person your parents disapprove of, or even if you've broken the law, no one has a right to punish you by making you have sex. If someone's spent money on you, taken you out, or given you presents, you don't owe him even as much as a kiss. Even if you've promised to make love and then changed your mind, you have a right to say no. Your body is not a bargaining chip and you are not for sale.

4. You have a right to be respected.

There is still a double standard in this country about boys, girls and sex. A boy who is sexually active early or who has many girlfriends is admired – he's seen as 'cool' and sexy. A girl who behaves in the same way is looked down upon, considered 'loose'. But girls have as much right as boys to be sexually active. No one should tell you he doesn't respect you because of your sexual activities, or pressurise you because of them. A boy who says, 'You did it with him, so why not with me?' should be told to get lost.

5. You have a right to say yes to some sexual activities and no to others.

Just because you've become physically intimate with someone doesn't mean you have to do anything you don't want. If you've almost gone all the way but haven't, you aren't obliged to. If you've made love with someone before, you aren't obliged to do so again. If you are willing to engage in some types of sexual activities but not others, you have a right to say so. If a boy tells you that you've gone too far to stop, don't believe him. Being frustrated might be unpleasant, but it won't hurt him.

This applies to boys, too, for sometimes girls will pressurise them into making love when they don't want to. For boys it can be especially difficult to refuse because you know you are supposed to be ready for sex whenever the opportunity arises; it isn't 'cool' to enjoy kissing but not want to make love. But you have as much right as anyone to set limits, to stop when you want and refuse what you don't want.

6. You have a right to have any sexual fantasies you want.

People often feel ashamed of the sexual fantasies they've had while daydreaming or masturbating. But you have a right to have any sexual fantasies you want without guilt. A lot of people feel especially guilty for having fantasies of rape or punishment, or for having sexual fantasies about people other than their boyfriend or girlfriend. Yet, fantasies like this are normal – everyone has them. Also, fantasising about something doesn't mean you really want it to happen. In a fantasy, you are in control because you are making up the story; in a rape the rapist is in control. In a fantasy, you feel desire; in a rape, you feel terror. In a fantasy, you are not in fear for your life; in a rape, you think you are going to be murdered. Your fantasies are your private affair.

Your sexual responsibilities

1. *You should always consider the feelings of your partner.*

    The key to happy lovemaking is considering the feelings of your partner. When you are sensitive to his or her moods, likes and dislikes, you can help build trust and relaxation between you - and that's good for being in love and making love. So if your partner is upset about something and wants to talk rather than kiss or make love, you should put your own wishes aside for the moment and tend to his or her needs.

2. *You should never pressurise someone to have sex.*

    Pressurising someone to have sex is pointless because no amount of pressure is going to create desire where there wasn't any before.

    If you are a boy, you should never try to force a girl to have sex with you. Even if you genuinely think a girl

intends to make love and are surprised when she won't, you shouldn't pressurise her.

Instead of trying to persuade her to make some kind of love with you, you should ask yourself a few questions: 'Why does she need persuading? Don't I turn her on? What would she like me to do? Doesn't she like me? Is she afraid? Perhaps she isn't ready yet?' You would build up a much better relationship with her if you found out the answers to some of these questions instead of pressurising her.

There are other kinds of pressures that both sexes sometimes use to force a person to have sex and these are equally important to avoid: being more popular at school, being older, being richer, having more experience, or having authority over someone. Even if a person is big and strong, he can, like the boy quoted below, be intimidated by these sorts of advantages into unwanted sex. This boy was so awed by the girl's superior age and experience, that he was afraid to say no.

My Mum had a friend over and she brought her daughter. Her daughter was an insane type ... she got mad and went out in the garden and took a bottle of vodka and drank the whole thing ... And then she came up to my room and she started doing this whole number on me ... I was really scared. I was petrified. I almost wanted to cry. She just started talking to me and all those other things, and we just had sex. It was always something I wanted to do, but I wanted to back out at the last minute with her...

To use any kind of advantage or physical pressure to force a person to have sex is assault.

3. *You should respect your partner.*

Sex can make you feel vulnerable, especially when you're new to it. That is why good sexual relations require trust between the partners. If a boy or girl has told you secrets, declared love for you, or made some kind of love with you, you should never make fun of him or her for it. When people have been intimate with you like that, they have made themselves vulnerable to you. Don't betray them.

4. Sex should be a mutual pleasure, never a punishment.

There are various ways in which men and women of all ages use sex inappropriately in this society. At one extreme is rape, when a man literally uses sex as an instrument of punishment and torture. On a more everyday level, both sexes sometimes use their sexual hold over someone to play power games. A girl might refuse sex with her boyfriend one night until he says he loves her, for instance. By doing this, she's using sex as a reward for something she forced out of him, and she's using the withholding of sex as a punishment. This is neither honest nor fair. A boy might do the same sort of thing, or he might force sex on a girl as a way of degrading her because he's angry with her or jealous. Using sex to manipulate people cheapens the act, ruins the pleasure, and destroys the chance of a good, loving relationship.

5. You should share the responsibility for birth control and sexual health with your partner.

Part of respecting someone and being considerate of his or her feelings is being concerned over the consequences of your sexual relationship together. With the increase of sexual diseases, especially AIDS (Acquired Immuno-Deficiency Syndrome), you have a right to know if your partner is healthy. And you have a responsibility to avoid sex if you have a sexual disease.

The responsibility for birth control also belongs to both partners. This means that before you have sex with someone, whether you are male or female, you bear the responsibility of bringing up the subject of contraception. It may not be the most romantic of openings, but 'Do you have any condoms?' is an essential question.

AIDS and Venereal Diseases. AIDS is an infection by the Human Immuno-Deficiency Virus, or HIV, which breaks down the body's immune system so that it cannot fight even the most common infections. HIV can be transmitted by the exchange of body fluids, so doctors advise sexually active people to use condoms above all other contraceptive devices, as a preventative of both AIDS and venereal diseases such as gonorrhea (usually known as 'the clap'), syphilis and herpes.

Whenever you are uncertain of your partner's complete sexual history, condoms are a must, and whether you are a boy or a girl, if you are sexually active, it is a very sensible idea to carry condoms with you.

Make sure you follow the instructions carefully, for to work as a protection against disease, the condom must prevent contact between the bodily fluids of the sexual partners. You should use lubricated condoms that have the spermicide nonoxyinol-9 in them (you should find it listed on the package). This spermicide is known to kill the HIV virus.

Birth control. If you have a regular sexual partner and know that you are safe from disease, condoms, the diaphagm or cap, or the pill are the safest methods of birth control. Contraceptives are available from your local Family Planning Clinic, and here you can obtain more advice and information about birth control and sexual diseases.

PROTECTING YOURSELF AMONG PEOPLE

It's very important to learn how to protect yourself during your daily life. And because sexual abuse is more likely to be directed against someone that the molester knows, the first thing to learn is how to protect yourself while going out with someone, at parties, at work, and in other social situations. These guidelines can help you become safer and freer to enjoy yourself without fear.

Decide right now what kind of intimacy you want with your partner. Don't leave the decision until the moment someone makes a move towards you; it's harder to resist when you have to decide on the spot. Think about the person you are going out with now. How much do you want to be touched by him or her? If you can work out your limits now, when you are alone and able to think calmly, you can make those limits clear when you have to.

Ask yourself if there is anyone you know at the moment who makes you feel uncomfortable. Is there someone who touches you too often, puts his or her hand on you, or always insists on kissing you hello even when you try to back off? Is there someone who always stands too close to you, or tries to get you to tell him or her intimate secrets about your life? Is there someone who likes to tease you or to make you embarrassed or uneasy?

If so, decide what you can do about it. Can you keep away from that person? If not, can you make it clear that you don't like what he or she is doing? If you stand up for yourself and say, 'Don't put your arm around me, it makes me uncomfortable,' or 'I'm sorry, but I'm not answering that question,' you might be able to stop the behaviour.

Make a deal with your parents: ask them to pick you up whenever you call them for help, wherever you are, without asking you questions and without getting angry with you. Even if it's late, you are somewhere you are not supposed to be, and you are drunk or even stoned, they should come to get you and promise not to get angry or to blame you for your predicament. Most of the time, you probably won't want to involve your parents in what you're doing, but just having them there as a safety valve can make you feel more secure. One mother made an arrangement like this with her teenage daughter:

If you find yourself with a boyfriend in his house late at night, he's trying to make you have sex when you don't want to and you can't get away, call me and I'll come. I won't embarrass you in front of him and I won't say anything about it for a whole day. Then we can sit down and talk about it.

If your parents won't agree to this arrangement, remind them that your safety should come first over everything. Tell them that a method like this was used in a town where many teenagers had been in drunk-driving accidents. Instead of driving when intoxicated the teenagers began calling their parents to pick them up. The rate of accidents dropped sharply.

Give your parents the parent's note in this book to read. It will show them how to help you be safer without intruding on your life.

Dates

'Date rape' – rape by boyfriends, dates and male friends - happens more frequently than is usually realised. Here you can learn how to protect yourself from date rape.

If you are a girl, be strong in your relationship with boys. Don't let your boyfriend always make the arrangements and decisions about where and when you go out - assert your own wants. And don't let him do all the paying, either, because that can give him a sense of power over you. Paying your own way makes you feel more independent and in control. When you come across as independent, you are less likely to be taken advantage of.

If you are a boy, don't feel that in order to be 'masculine' you have to make all the decisions and do all the paying. That idea is outdated and sexist. When relationships are more equal, both partners are less likely to feel used.

If you go out with someone you don't know well, stay in public places. If you are a girl, you will feel safer this way. If you are a boy, you will have the chance to get to know your date gradually and in a more relaxed way.

Think about what you expect from a relationship. How far are you willing to go sexually right now? How well do you want to know someone before you start any sexual activity? How do you want to feel about a person before you make love for the first time? What sorts of feelings do you want a person to have about you before you make love for the first time?

Once you know your limits, stick to them. Make it clear to your boyfriend or girlfriend from the outset what you will and won't do. If you are a virgin, for

instance, and want to stay that way, tell your friend as soon as the relationship gets sexual. If you are a girl and a boy starts doing something you don't want, like putting his hand on your breast, make him stop right away. If the boy cares about you and respects your wishes, he will stop. If you are a boy, don't feel you have to press ahead sexually until the girl stops you; ask her how far she wants to go if she won't tell you initially. And think about how far you really want to go, too. It's much more pleasant to know what to expect than to be waiting anxiously for her to stop you at any minute.

Never let anyone force you into being alone with him or her against your will. Be firm from the start and say, 'No thanks, I don't want to go there.' If the person ignores these refusals and tries to bully you, get away from him or her and think about whether you want to stay with someone that pushy.

If you are a girl, don't pretend to reject a boy sexually if you don't mean it. It confuses a boy, which isn't fair to him, and leads him to believe the myth that women never mean it when they say 'no'.

If you are going out with a boy who has a reputation for 'scoring,' be prepared for him to try to pressurise you into sex.

If you are dating a girl who is used to having sex with her boyfriends, don't assume she expects the same from you. Don't pressurise a girl to have sex just because you know she's had it before, and at the same time try not to get hung up about 'performing' or being as 'good' as her other boyfriends. Making love concerns only the two of you.

If your boyfriend or girlfriend is old enough to drive, and you like to go out in a car, avoid stopping in isolated areas. Places like lovers' lanes and country fields can be dangerous. Choose an area where lots of couples go, or find a populated place where you can have both privacy and safety, like down a side street.

How to Handle Sexual Assault by a Date

This section is aimed at girls, for boys are rarely, if ever, assaulted by a girl on a date. Boys are in more danger from gangs of other boys and from older men and women.

If a boy demands sex from you and won't take no for an answer, no matter how firm you are, that's assault. Assess the situation. Can you run away or call for help? How far from people are you? Can you attract attention? Can you use the self-defence methods described in chapter seven?

If you can't find an alternative, try to talk your way to safety. Say something like 'Look, you don't have to get angry. I just need to relax first. I know somewhere more comfortable we could go.' Then try to get him back to a party with you, to a friend's house – anywhere public. You could even say you want to eat first, or you need a drink or a cigarette to relax, and you know someone who could get you one. If you can make him think you want to have sex with him so that he doesn't force you, you can then lure him somewhere public so that you can escape. Some people have escaped rape by claiming they needed to go to the bathroom first, then locking themselves in and crawling out of the window or calling for help.

These kinds of tricks can work because the boy wants to believe that you are attracted to him – it's good for his ego. If you pretend to be willing, you are turning the situation away from an assault into a seemingly normal sexual encounter - until you trick the boy and escape.

Once you have escaped, don't delude yourself into thinking things will be any different on the next date. Never go out with him again.

If you are assaulted by a date, don't keep it a secret. This applies even if the attack wasn't successful. Tell your parents or a trusted adult and discuss whether or not to tell a school authority, the boy's family, or the police. The boy needs to be stopped before he hurts someone else. What is more, you owe it to yourself to get help handling something as traumatic as this; you shouldn't have to do it on your own.

Reporting an assault not only protects yourself and other possible victims, but can help the offender. A boy often molests because he himself is being molested. When the girls in one school decided to tell about a boy who'd been harassing them, pupils, parents and staff were all grateful.

Several girls in the school reported that one of the boys was exposing himself to them on the playground. He was also phoning them in the evening and telling them that he was masturbating while he talked to them. The boy was interviewed by counsellors and teachers, then a three-hour meeting was held with his parents to help them understand what was going on, why it was happening, and what could be done to help. They were very thankful to be able to intervene before their son moved on to doing worse things, and they were concerned that someone might be abusing him.

Parties and Groups

Although staying with groups of people you know is one of the best ways of keeping safe, sometimes groups can get dangerous. Here are some ways to protect yourself:

If you're going to a party, try to arrange your transport home beforehand. Relying on strangers and acquaintances for lifts home is dangerous. Many so-called 'date rapes' and 'acquaintance rapes' are committed by boys who offer a ride home to a girl they have just met. Call your parents instead, get a taxi, ask a friend to come home and stay with you, or arrange to go home with a friend and stay with her.

I'd been at this party till pretty late, and it was time to go. I didn't have a way of getting home without spending a lot of money on a taxi, so this bloke I'd just met at the party offered to walk me home. He was a friend of one of my friends, so I said OK. We walked along some dark roads, then he suddenly grabbed me and pulled me into the bushes. He raped me.

Don't go to empty houses or wild parties with people you don't know.

If you are with people you don't know, avoid getting very drunk or even stoned. You need to keep your wits about you.

Whenever you're with a group that includes people you don't know well, avoid going off alone with any one or more of the boys. This is true at parties, too. Especially avoid going to isolated areas in parks, country lanes, or houses.

If you get high on drugs or drink when you're out, don't go home alone. This applies day or night. You look – and are – especially vulnerable when you are intoxicated, even though you may feel stronger, more daring, and safer.

Don't be embarrassed to turn down lifts from a person you don't like. If you don't trust him, you feel odd about him in any way, or he has been drinking or taking drugs, turn down the lift. Trust your instincts; very often they prove valid.

If you are uneasy in someone's car, sit in the back, make sure the car door unlocks and the seat belt unfastens, and be ready to jump out if you have to. If you follow the suggestions above, though, you should never find yourself in this situation.

How to Handle Dangerous Group Situations

Sometimes parties can turn violent or become dangerous.
If there's any physical violence, leave immediately.

telephone

Act confident. If there is some kind of cruel teasing going on, you are less likely to be picked on if you don't look scared.

Pay attention to your instincts. If the situation gets threatening, someone starts insulting someone else, people start ganging up against someone – the sooner you act, the better. Don't hang around hoping things will improve – leave. And get help if the trouble looks serious.

If things are really out of hand and you can't run to get help, do something unexpected. Turn the lights on and off suddenly, turn the music way up or off, break a window, ring the doorbell, shout out that the police are coming. You might save someone from being hurt, assaulted or raped.

If you see that someone at a party is about to get attacked, either sexually or in a fight, don't just stand around doing nothing. Appeal to a friend to help you stop it, if possible, or leave and call the police from the privacy of another room, from a neighbour's house, or from a street phone. Whether you are a boy whose friends are warming up to a gang assault, or a girl whose friends want to smash up a house, think how bad you'll feel if you go along with them against your will. Don't be like this boy:

When I was at school, I went to a party once in my home town. It was late and everyone was high on something. I heard a commotion inside the house and I asked someone what was going on. They said a retarded girl was being gang-banged. I didn't know what to do or how to stop it, so I didn't do anything.

Job Interviews, Newspaper Rounds, Summer Jobs

If you are going to a job interview at the house of someone you don't know, take a parent or a friend who can wait for you outside.

If any job makes you feel uneasy or scared, don't ignore those feelings – work out why. Does your employer make you feel uneasy? Or is it one of the customers? Are you being looked at or treated in a way that is threatening or unpleasant? If you feel in danger, leave.

Don't take a job that puts you in a vulnerable position. For example, it isn't safe for you to work in a shop by yourself.

Let your parents know where your job is and make sure they'll agree to come and get you if you ever need help or a lift home.

Don't take a job delivering newspapers in an area you don't know or don't feel safe in. If you must, get to know the area and find out from people living there which are the safest streets. Follow the safety rules in the next chapter, 'Protecting Yourself Outside'.

How to Handle Trouble From People in Authority

Many people are intimidated by authority figures: employers, parents, doctors, teachers, coaches, and for young people, almost any adult. It can be hard to stand up to a person in authority if he or she does something wrong to you. You have trouble saying no because you are used to obeying that person. You might be afraid no one would believe you if you told on him or her. Or that person might threaten to tell embarrassing stories about you, get you into trouble, or take revenge on you. It is important to be able to look up to and admire someone, but when a person abuses his or her power over you by molesting you in any way, that person no longer deserves your respect. Here are some examples of situations like this and what to do about them.

Employers

Employers sometimes abuse their power over you with what is known as 'sexual harassment'. This can mean asking you inappropriately intimate questions about your love life, your body, or your social life - questions like 'Do you have sex?' 'Do you sleep with your boy/girlfriend?' If the person persists and won't take your hints that you don't like it, that constitutes sexual harassment.

Sexual harassment can also mean making passes at you, making suggestions that you do something sexual (like posing nude for photographs), or trying to get a date with you. And it can mean actually molesting you, too.

Sarah got a job one summer working as a waitress in a popular cafe. But her boss, a man in his forties with a wife and three kids, wouldn't leave her alone. He flirted with her, touched her all the time, and, worst of all, pinched her behind whenever she walked by him. She didn't say anything because she noticed he did this to the other waitresses too, but it made her summer miserable.

Sarah thought that the other waitresses didn't mind her boss's behaviour and was so intimidated by this idea that she didn't stand up for herself. Probably every waitress in the place felt the same way. If they had talked among themselves, they could have worked out how to stop their boss. They could have confronted him and asked him to stop touching them;

they could have threatened to strike; or they could have arranged for each one to ask him privately to stop. As a last resort, they could all have walked out on him at once.

A lot of adults and teenagers put up with sexual harassment because they are afraid of losing their job. You have to decide for yourself how bad you are being made to feel and whether this job is worth it, and also how much danger you might be in. But meanwhile, try these tactics:

◆ *Tell your boss that you prefer to keep your outside life private.*

◆ *Tell them you want to be left alone. If their approaches have been mild and you are polite but firm, they might get the message.*

◆ *Remember your sexual rights: you have a right not to put up with anyone who makes you feel scared, humiliated, or ashamed.*

Once a boss has sexually molested you or threatened to, you must not only leave the job, you must tell your parents and even the police. What they are doing is illegal, and you have to protect other teenagers as well as yourself.

Doctors

Doctors are another group of people who have authority and power over you. Abuse of this authority is extremely serious and should be recognised and confronted. Remember, you have rights to privacy and respect and if these rights are being infringed don't be afraid to act.

If you ever feel uncomfortable with a doctor, let him or her and other people know it.

If a doctor molests you in any way, tell your parents and demand that he or she be reported to the hospital administrator (if you are in hospital), the police, or the Family Practitioners' Committee.

Teachers, Coaches, Youth Leaders etc.

Molesters who take jobs as teachers, athletic coaches, scout leaders, or youth organisers are counting on three things to prevent you from telling on them: your fear of them, your guilt, and your worry that no one would believe you even if you did tell.

They tend to reinforce the first - your fear of them - with threats like these: 'I'll fail you,' 'I'll tell your parents that you never come to school,' 'I'll report your behaviour to the headmaster.'

Always remember that, whatever you've done, their molesting is worse. Any parent or adult should know this, so you should never be afraid to tell a trusted adult what is happening.

Sometimes, the molester will stop at nothing to get you to keep quiet, and he may make threats against you. In a case like this, it's especially important to get the help of an adult. If no one you know seems suitable - they'll be too shocked or too angry or too scared - go to a Rape Crisis Centre or a child abuse agency for help. (See chapter nine, 'Sources of Safety' for the addresses and phone numbers of places to turn to.)

Molesters prey on the second factor, your guilt, by telling you the abuse was your fault. They might say things like 'You're no good, so you deserve it,' or enlist you in some shameful activity, like looking at or buying pornography, so that you feel too guilty to tell on them. Again, try to remember that, no matter what you've done, the abuse is never your fault. You are being manipulated and used, and you have a right to get help.

The third factor that molesters count on, that no one would believe you if you told, can be countered by taking these steps:

Start by telling a close friend about the abuse. If you have a friend to help you tell adults, or to go with you to a crisis centre, telling can be much easier.

Next, ask around among your friends to see if any of them have been molested by this person, too. If the molester is the father of one of your friends, a teacher, or someone else who has contact with lots of kids, the odds are quite high he is molesting more people than just you. If several of you report him at once, adults will be more likely to believe you.

After that, tell someone in your family whom you trust. If you don't think you can tell your mother or father about the assaults yet, think of another adult you like instead - a teacher, perhaps; your best friend's mother; an aunt. That adult can help you break the news to your parents. There is more about the difficulties of telling in chapter eight.

Finally, if you are sure that you can't tell anyone you know, follow the advice in chapter eight and call a help organisation or child abuse centre.

Older Friends

If an older friend tries to engage you in any kind of sex, you have a right to resist in any way you need to. Say, 'No! I'll tell my mother,' 'I'll tell the whole team,' 'I'll tell the whole school.' If that doesn't work, you have the right to resist physically. See chapter seven, 'Self-Defence,' for how to do this. You also have a right and a duty to tell a trusted adult immediately in order to stop the molester from finding another victim. He may be a paedophile: he may depend on teenagers for friendship and for sex. Ask around to see if other teenagers have complaints about him, too, and make sure he is reported to the police. Chapter eight will tell you what to do if you don't want to report him because you are afraid, embarrassed, or you like him too much.

How To Handle Sexual Abuse By A Parent

If you have a parent who tries to sexually assault you, you may be able to protect yourself with verbal and even physical resistance, but usually you will need outside interference by other adults or the law. A lot of young people try to solve the problem by running away, but that usually only creates other problems.

Being molested by a parent is one of the most devastating traumas possible. The very people who are supposed to protect you from such things are committing them. It makes you feel that your home is no longer safe, that no one loves or ever will love you, and that you can't ever trust anyone in the world. If you have been sexually abused over a long time by someone in your family, you probably think of yourself as different from anyone else you know. You feel alone, burdened by a shameful secret, and you might look on yourself as somehow dirty and inferior to everyone else. You may also be full of hatred - for the molester, for the rest of the family for not rescuing you, even for yourself. You may, like this teenage victim of incest, try endlessly to find reasons to blame yourself for the assault, as if you were the criminal:

I would sit for hours on end and try to think of why this happened to me. I thought of every mistake, every lie, every bad feeling I ever had towards another person. I thought I was being punished for something, but I couldn't think of exactly why.

Try to remember that you are not alone. Hundreds and thousands of children have been sexually abused by their relatives and parents. And try to remember that the assaults didn't happen because of anything you did, who you are, or what you are like. It is the molesters' hangups, their problems, and their selfishness that made them abuse you. There are people who will help you. There are solutions to find. But you have to tell someone what is happening. Keeping it a secret allows your parent to keep doing it to you and maybe to your sisters or brothers as well. Keeping it a secret also means your parent will never get the help they need to stop their behaviour.

In chapter seven, 'Self-Defence', you will find advice on what to say to stop a parent assaulting you, and what to do physically if you must. In chapter eight, 'Getting Help', there is advice on who to tell, how to find help, and what will happen when you do. Never forget that you deserve all the help you can get.

PROTECTING YOURSELF OUTSIDE

Self-defence begins with how you look and feel. If you stand and
move with confidence, look danger in the eye, and appear
alert, you are already frightening off some potential assailants.
This chapter will teach you to look confident, to trust your
instincts, and to look after yourself out in the streets.

Basic Rules

◆ *Trust Your Feelings*

The golden rule of self-defence is to pay attention to and trust your
instincts. Countless victims of sexual assault and other crimes
have said, 'I felt something was wrong, but I didn't want to look
stupid, so I didn't do anything.' If you feel uncomfortable around
a person or a place, if a warning signal goes off somewhere deep
inside you, if you feel scared or even just uneasy, don't ignore it. It
is always better to act on your warning instincts and never know
whether you were right than to ignore them and find yourself a
victim; a moment of looking foolish is nothing compared to
being assaulted. Take the story of these two teenage girls:

*We were walking home from school to my house,
which was empty, when we heard a man behind us.
We both got scared that he was following us, so we
did our self-defence yell and ran to a neighbour's
house, where we knew someone was home.*

Those girls never knew whether they were in danger or not,
but by not waiting around to find out, they avoided even
taking a risk.

◆ **Look Alert**

Research has shown that muggers don't necessarily pick girls
over boys, women over men, or old people over young
people, as you might expect. They go for people who look
vulnerable because of the way they walk: people
who look uncoordinated, as if they are in
a daze or lost, and who walk hunched
over and with bad posture, paying no
attention to their surroundings.

Anyone out to attack someone on the
street is nervous, doesn't want to get
caught, and doesn't want to get
hurt, so he picks someone who
literally looks like a pushover.
You can easily avoid looking like
that yourself by standing up
straight, keeping you feet slightly apart for
good balance, and keeping your head up
and your mind focused on what's going on
around you. If you look alert and aware,
people will be less likely to pick on
you.

◆ *Don't Handicap Yourself*

Part of being alert is avoiding doing and wearing things that make you look especially vulnerable. Personal stereos, for example, make you a walking target because the headphones block out your sense of hearing and make you less alert. Try to avoid getting absorbed in a book, a newspaper, or a map out on the street; don't stand with your head buried in a bag looking for something, or fall asleep in public places. Above all, think about the way you dress.

Wobbly or high heels, tight skirts, and any other clothes that hinder your movement are not a good idea if you're planning to walk somewhere. Wide-brimmed hats, hoods, sunglasses and umbrellas can obscure your vision and make you more vulnerable, so choose those carefully and be extra alert when you're using them. And loading yourself down with packages or books or a heavy bag is a bad idea, too. If you want to dress up for a party, but you have to walk or take public transport, change into party clothes once you're there. And remember, if you need to carry a bag, don't wind it around your hand or arm – that makes it too easy for someone to pull you over.

Safety in the Street

When you leave home, carry your keys separately from your purse, wallet, identification, and address. That way, if you lose keys or something with your address on it, you won't risk giving a criminal access to your house.

When you're out, always have enough money for a phone call. Money for a bus or taxi is a good idea, too. Some people who live in high-crime areas always make sure they carry some money in case they are mugged - muggers occasionally get so infuriated if their victims have nothing that they hurt them out of anger.

Know where you are going. If you are somewhere unfamiliar, work out your route before you leave so that you won't get or look lost.

Don't take shortcuts through car parks, alleyways, or other isolated areas, especially if you are alone.

Avoid vacant buildings, and sparsely populated streets.

Walk in the middle of the pavement. Stay away from entrances to houses and alleyways.

Don't wait in a car alone in a car park or garage. If you do find yourself in a car alone and feel at all uneasy, lock the doors and put the windows up most of the way. If anyone you don't know approaches, don't unlock the doors or put the windows down.

If you go to the same place every day - to and from school, for instance - try to vary the route you take. Choose different streets once in a while, or meet a friend on the way there or back for a change. This can foil anyone who might have been watching you.

If you live in a city, be aware which streets have shops and good lighting. If you live in the suburbs or in a small town, know which streets have houses where people are usually at home, and which ones have plenty of streetlights. That way, you'll know where to go should you ever feel scared or need help.

If you jog, try not to go alone. Choose a busy area and time of day, pay attention to your surroundings, avoid woods and isolated areas, don't use a personal stereo, and keep the last part of the run, when you are most tired, for the safest place.

If you see a group of men or boys on the street, don't walk through them. Cross the street, go around them, or even double back and choose another street.

Try to avoid walking anywhere or taking transport alone at night. Share a taxi home with friends instead, or ask your parents to pick you up.

It's a good idea to carry a personal attack alarm in your pocket. You can use this to startle an attacker, and to give you time to escape.

You are no safer on bicycle than on foot. Don't bike where you wouldn't walk, and follow the safety rules above.

How to Handle Harassment, Flashers and Other Assaults

◆ *If You Are Harassed On The Street*

Most of the time, the men who shout at you in the street don't intend to do you any physical harm. But if you feel at all afraid, or you are in a deserted place, pretend you didn't hear the remarks, don't talk back, and don't get physically close to the harasser. Walk away briskly with your head held high, looking confident and unworried. Remember, anyone who gets a kick out of shouting at women in the street is proving himself a coward. By not responding to him, you are being dignified, not afraid.

It's better not to shout obscenities or get into a verbal fight – that will only prolong the unpleasantness and might, in rare circumstances, provoke physical violence. But if you can answer calmly and with conviction, you may, like this girl below, have the satisfaction of refusing to be a passive victim to this kind of everyday abuse.

I was walking down the street feeling happy, when two workmen began shouting obscene things at me. Their intrusion on my mood and my privacy made me furious. So I stopped and shouted at them, 'I have as much right to walk down the street without getting hassled as you do! Leave me alone!' They stood there

*for several seconds with their mouths hanging open
before they remembered to be cool and laugh. I was
embarrassed afterwards, but I felt satisfied, too.*

Pretending not to see an exhibitionist is the safest reaction, even
though it can be frustrating – you'd probably rather find some
way to humiliate him. Get away from him as fast as possible,
and if he's hanging around other young people, report him to a
teacher, your parents, or anyone else suitable. If you know
where he tends to hang out, telling the police is a good idea,
too.

◆ If You Are Being Followed On Foot or By Car

If you think you're
being followed, don't
dismiss your fear as
paranoia – act. Turn
around and look.
Cross the street. On a
main street, stop and
look in a shop
window, using it as a
mirror to watch the
person you suspect. If
he persists in following
you, run into a shop
or a neighbour's house and call a parent or a friend to come
and get you. Don't run off into deserted side streets, or
anywhere that is isolated and dangerous – if you can't find
anywhere safe to run to, return the way you came, making
sure you don't pass within grabbing distance of the follower.
If you are really scared, go to the nearest house that has
people at home and ask them to call your parents and the
police. Never be afraid to ask for help. As this fourteen-year-

old boy decided, there's never any point in risking your safety
out of pride or the fear of looking foolish:

*I was walking home with a pizza one night when
some guys shouted, 'Hey, come over here!' I didn't like
the look of them, so I shouted back, 'I can't, I've got
to deliver this pizza.' They crossed the street and
started coming at me, so I went in a shop and asked
two women in there if they'd walk me home. They did,
and I was OK.*

If you notice a car following you beside the kerb and you are in
a city or town, run across the street and towards a busy,
populated area as quickly as possible. If you are on a deserted
country road, get off the road and run to a house, or hide
somewhere you know no one could find you, like up a tree.
Don't go deep into woods or fields unless you know a secret
way home that no one else could find. Never lead anyone
who is following you to your home.

◆ *If You Are Mugged*

Most muggers only want your money. Most of them are also
scared. That's why you should never fight any mugger who
has a weapon, is with other people, can clearly overpower
you, or seems liable to panic and hurt you in any way. Your
physical safety is never worth a wallet or a watch. Some
muggers, however, are also potential rapists, and that's also
why you should never antagonise one. If you are mugged,
keep calm by taking steady breaths, tell the man exactly
what valuables you have on you and where they are (don't
try to hide anything because if he finds it, he might get
angry and hurt you). Then hand them over, moving slowly,
and telling him exactly what you are doing: 'I am taking my
wallet out of my pocket.' Look at his face, not at the weapon

– it makes you seem calmer, which will help him not to panic (unless of course, he expressly tells you not to look at him). Remember, he is scared, too – if you can keep calm, you can help to calm him. Don't appear contemptuous, don't beg or plead, and don't provoke him.

If a mugger tries to make you go somewhere more isolated with him, like a car or a car park, or if he tries to force you into your home, you have a more dangerous situation on your hands. See chapter seven, 'Self-Defence,' for ways to prevent this.

◆ If You Are Jostled or Otherwise Bothered

There are several ways in which assailants of all kinds try to test out potential victims on the street: they bump into you, they purposely block your way, they walk right up to you, or stand unnaturally close to you in a crowd, they look you up and down and appear to enjoy your discomfort, or they start talking to you as if they know you really well. If any of these things happen, move away quickly and walk off without showing fear or shock. Look firm but not frightened, as if you're thinking, I know what you're up to, but you're not going to bother me. Make your face as expressionless as possible, and don't make any comment. This way you will look alert, dignified and tough.

◆ If Someone Offers or Asks for Help

If a stranger offers to help you carry packages or to give you a lift, stand tall and confident and say, 'No thank you.' Then walk away briskly.

A trick that both muggers and rapists have been known to use is to work in pairs: one person intimidates you on the street, the other one pretends he's a kind stranger and offers to walk you somewhere safe. The pair can be two men or a man and a woman. If this happens, say no firmly and get away fast. If the 'helper' persists, run into a shop and get help, or do the self-defence yell (described in chapter seven) and run.

If someone asks you for directions, don't go too close to them, especially if they are in a car. Either say 'Sorry, I don't know' and keep walking if you don't like the look of them, or shout your directions from a distance as if you are in a hurry to get somewhere.

A man once beckoned me over to his car, waving a map as if he was lost. I went over and looked in. He was masturbating.

If the people asking directions are a family, there's probably no need to be suspicious. But be wary of lone men, men in groups, and even couples.

If a man or woman comes up to you on the street and asks for help, or you see someone lying down and groaning, there are ways to help without putting yourself in unnecessary danger. Offer to phone the police or an ambulance from the nearest phone booth but don't get too close to the person and don't accompany them to an isolated area; it could be a trick. You'll have to use your own judgement on this, of course, because if you think someone's really hurt, you may choose to risk being tricked in order to help. If the person refuses your offer to call for help, however, he or she may not be as badly off as you think.

◆ If You Have To Turn To A Stranger For Help

Once, when I was being followed, I stopped a young man on the street and told him what was happening. I asked him to walk with me for a block as if he knew me, in the hope it would frighten the creep off. The man said, 'I don't have time. Why don't you cut through that car park?' Not only was I shocked at his unwillingness to help even though I was in danger, but I realised he'd made a suggestion that would have put me in even more danger.

Unfortunately, relying on strangers for help has its risks, too – they might take advantage of your vulnerability and attack you themselves. You should take these precautions: If you go into a shop for help or to use the phone, stay in the public area. Don't go into a back room or a basement with someone you don't know. Insist on calling your parents or the police, rather than taking a lift from a stranger. Don't take suggestions that are contrary to the advice in this book.

Safety In Public Places

If you like to hang around in parks, on the beach, in arcades, fast food places, shopping precincts, or any other open, public place, take these precautions:

◆ *Stay with your friends, or at least within sight of them.*

◆ *Avoid these places at night, especially if they tend to be deserted or to attract gangs.*

◆ *Avoid deserted toilets. Go with a friend.*

Keep an eye out for lone adults, especially men or older boys, who hang about in places where young people congregate. I you notice a man on his own hovering around trying to make friends with you, your friends, or younger children, ask yourself why he isn't with people his own age. If he tries to make friends with you, or he offers you money, food, drink, or drugs, refuse and act cold and distant. If he persists, or you see him playing a lot with a particular child, tell the shopkeepers in the arcade, your parents, or another trusted adult about him: he could be a molester. You could try to warn the children, too, or even call their parents if you know them.

If you want to go for a long walk in the park or in the country by yourself, think about how safe you'll feel and what you could do if you were attacked. How near would you be to houses or streets where you could get help? Do you know your way out of the park, or your way home? No amount of self-defence awareness should make you feel that you can't enjoy the countryside. But at the same time, you should be cautious. If your local park is known to be unsafe at certain hours, don't go in at those times. If you go off on a walk, make sure someone knows where you are going and when you expect to be back.

Safety While Travelling

Whether you are going on a special holiday or just taking the bus to school, here are some safety tips you should know and follow:

◆ *Stay alert while waiting for a bus or train. Be aware of what is going on around you, and, if you are in a dangerous area, stand with your back to the wall so you can't be approached from behind. Never stand on the edge of a train platform or within reach of a passing train.*

◆ *Avoid isolated bus stops and train stations, if*

possible, especially in cities and at night.

◆ *Get your money ready in your hand so that you don't have to fumble around with your head buried in a wallet or bag.*

◆ *Sit near the driver or conductor if the train or bus is empty, or if there are suspicious-looking people around you.*

◆ *If you're on holiday in a place you don't know well, ask people you know which areas to avoid and which streets are the busiest and safest. Study the map before you go out - not on the street - and learn your way around so that you don't look lost and bewildered.*

◆ *DON'T hitchhike. Convicted rapists have told interviewers that they see hitchhikers as ready-made victims and even go looking for them when they want to rape. Boys are often victimised this way because they think it's safe for them to hitchhike. Hitching is so dangerous, with a friend or without, that the adventure of it simply isn't worth the risk.*

If you absolutely must hitch, here are some essential precautions: Trust your instincts and never get into a car with anyone who makes you feel uneasy in any way. Don't get into a car that has more than one man in it. Sit in the back. Make sure the door is unlocked. Keep your luggage with you at all times. Before you get in, look for door handles – if there aren't any, don't get in. If you are with a friend, don't let yourselves get separated into the front and back seats. If you are a boy hitching with a girlfriend, she should get in last and get out first. Don't accept lifts with people who are intoxicated. And don't think that if you are in another country you are automatically safe.

Even if you take all these precautions, you are still at risk. When you are making yourself as vulnerable as you are when you hitch, you can't trust anyone.

How To Handle Trouble While Travelling

◆ *If Someone Molests You*

I was on the subway in rush hour, and a man started putting his hand up my skirt. I was so shocked that I couldn't do anything, but just stood there while his hand crept higher and higher. I kept wondering, 'Can anyone see? Do they think I like this?' and hoping someone would help me. Ever since, I've felt ashamed every time I think of it, because I just stood there doing nothing.

A lot of people react to being molested like that - they freeze. If anyone rubs up against you, touches you up, or exposes himself to you on a bus or train, move away immediately. Go to the driver or conductor and complain. If there are people around you, shout, 'This man is bothering me!' or 'There's a pervert in here!' and get away from him. Make sure the man doesn't follow you off the bus or train and if he does, follow the suggestions below.

◆ *If You Are Being Watched or Followed*

If you catch someone staring at you, look directly at him for a second. Don't stare or engage in any prolonged eye contact, but just let him know you've seen him. If anyone who's been bothering you looks as if he's about to follow you off the bus or train, step back and let him get off first, then stay on to the next stop. If he doesn't get off, stay on until you get to a stop near shops and a phone, so you can ring your parents and ask them to come and get you.

Whenever you are being followed, don't go straight home. Go to a shop, or a friend or neighbour's house (if possible), and call for help. And always stay in a populated area.

◆ *If Someone Talks To You Persistently*

I was stuck on a train once during a breakdown, and this middle-aged man started chatting to me. I didn't like him because he was pushy, so I acted cold and moved away from him. He got the message, but then he turned to this young teenage girl and started talking to her. She was too embarrassed to be rude to him, and pretty soon he was touching her earrings and necklace and asking her about her boyfriends and making her blush. She looked embarrassed, because everyone could hear.

Don't let someone intimidate you into putting up with pushy, personal, or unpleasant conversation. If he's insensitive enough to keep bothering you, you don't have to worry about being rude to him. If brief, cold answers and a turned-away head don't stop him, pointedly moving away from him should. If you are absolutely stuck next to him in a rush-hour crowd, shout, 'There's a man bothering me here, please let me through.' Make sure he's the one who is embarrassed, not you.

Safety Coming Home

Coming into your home, especially if you live in a block of flats, can be dangerous. Muggers and rapists sometimes choose to hide and ambush people in lobbies, hallways, and doorways because they are hidden from the street. Here are some precautions you can take:

If you live in a block of flats, arrange a safety code ring with your family. Then, if you are stuck downstairs with someone you are afraid of, you can ring your door bell in the pre-arranged code. That way, anyone at home will know to call the police and come down to help you.

Always have your keys in your hand before you approach your front door. Fumbling for keys in a hidden doorway makes it easy for an offender to attack you or force you in with him.

If someone unfamiliar is hanging around your hallway, don't go in. Walk past. Wait. Phone home from a phone booth if someone is there who could come and get you. Go to a local shop or a neighbourhood friend for help.

As you enter the hallway of a block of flats, look behind you quickly, and make sure no one is hiding around a corner. Shut the door quickly behind you. If you see anyone, get back out of the building as soon as possible and go to a phone to call for help.

A person who enters your block of flats with a key in his hand doesn't necessarily live there. If you've never seen that person before, let him go in first - if he can't unlock the door or he tries to make you unlock it for him, pretend you've forgotten something and leave.

Don't let anyone into your building or house you don't know. This is difficult when you want to be polite, but too many offenders gain access to homes this way. Either pretend you don't see the person if he or she comes up behind you as you enter, and close the door quickly behind you, or ask them to ring the bell of the person they are visiting. If the person insists, be firm or just end the conversation by walking away and leaving them outside the locked door. Any decent visitor would respect your caution.

If you find your door open or unlocked when you get home and it shouldn't be, don't go in. You don't want to surprise thieves in the act; they may turn violent. Instead, go to a neighbour's, call the police, and call your parents, then wait for the police to arrive and let them go in before you. Never confront a burglar. A scared burglar is a dangerous burglar.

If you come home alone and feel scared for any reason, stand by the door and yell something like 'I'm home!' and wait until you hear a response. If no one in your family answers, or if you still feel scared, don't go in. Go to a friend's instead, or ask a neighbour you don't know well to go in with you. Sometimes people's instincts tell them that an intruder is in their home. If you habitually feel scared coming home alone, talk to your parents about what can be done to make you feel safer.

6

PROTECTING YOURSELF INSIDE

Many sexual attacks occur inside or near the victim's home, just where most people feel the safest. Many others happen in places we normally consider safe, too, like school or a friend's house. Here are some ways to keep yourself safer inside.

Safety At Home Alone

When you are at home alone, take the following precautions:

Leave a few lights on around the house so you don't look as if you're by yourself.

Always close curtains and blinds at night. That way, people won't be able to watch you.

Lock the doors behind you when you are inside.

Avoid going to deserted areas of a building alone. This includes the basement, laundry room, and roof.

If you live in a block of flats never let in someone you don't know or expect. Always use the intercom to ask who it is, and be sure you recognise the voice. If someone says, 'It's me,' ask, 'Who's me?' If there is no intercom, arrange a code ring with friends so that you know it's not a stranger at the door.

Don't open the door to anyone you don't know. Always use a spyhole if you have one to make sure you recognise the person.

If you are home alone and someone knocks or rings at the door, follow these steps:

◆ *Ask who it is through the door.*

◆ *If you don't know or trust the person, ask him or her to come back later. You could say,' My parents are busy right now.'*

◆ *If it's a delivery, ask the person to leave it on the doorstep. If they have a paper for you to sign, tell them to slip it under the door. Anyone genuine will respect your caution.*

◆ *If it's a repair person, ask to see an identity card and call the company to make sure they really sent the person to your house. If the person at your door is an imposter, they'll probably go away as soon as they realise you are checking on them. A lot of assailants have found their way into homes*

*by posing as repairmen. Some of them even have
uniforms.*

◆ *Never give your address to anyone you don't know,
in person or on the phone.*

◆ *NEVER REVEAL THAT YOU ARE ALONE.*

Criminals are very resourceful about thinking of ways to get
into your house. Beware of cons such as people asking for
help in an emergency. Offer to phone for the police or an
ambulance, but follow the rules above and don't open the
door to a stranger.

How To Handle Attempted and Actual Break-ins

If someone at your door won't go away even when you use the
precautions described above, phone your neighbours and the
police immediately. Make sure your doors and windows are
locked, too.

If you hear someone break into the house,
remember - DON'T CONFRONT A
BURGLAR. Try to get out by
another exit immediately, run to a
neighbour, and call the police. If you
can't get out, lock yourself in a room,
ring the police if you can, and try
to escape through a
window if you can do
so safely.

If you see a strange car parked in
front of your house and any evidence that
there's been a break-in, DON'T GO IN. Take
the registration number, go to a neighbour's,
and call the police.

If you see a Peeping Tom (someone who watches you through a window or door, hoping you won't see him), lock your doors and windows immediately and call the police. Call a neighbour, too, and ask them to come over.

How to Handle Suspicious or Obscene Phone Calls

If you get an obscene, silent, or heavy-breathing call, hang up immediately but calmly. Be prepared for the caller to try again. If he does, either get your father or brother with an adult voice to answer a few times, or don't answer the phone at all. If the caller persists over several days, tap the phone with a pen, as if the call is being traced. Try not to talk about the calls to friends and acquaintances - obscene callers are often people who know you, and to hear that you are distressed is just what they need to keep wanting to bother you. Finally, if the caller won't give up, call the police and the phone company for further advice and help. You may have to change your phone number.

If someone calls up and says, 'Guess who this is,' don't. Say, 'I don't play guessing games on the phone. Say who you are or I'll hang up,' and hang up immediately if the person won't identify himself or herself.

If someone calls up and says, 'Who is this?' or 'Is this ...' and lists your number, don't give them the answer they want. Say, 'Who's calling, please?' and 'Who are you trying to reach?' Make them identify themselves before saying who you are. Criminals often try to find out where you live with these tricks.

If a person you don't know calls and asks to speak to your parents, don't let on that you are home alone. Say, 'My mother's busy; can I take a message?'

Never give anyone you don't know personal information on

the phone. A common ruse of burglars and other criminals is to pose as people doing a survey, or some kind of market research firm. Before you know it, you are being asked about your daily habits, where you live, and your sex life. No real survey about sexuality would ask you questions on the phone at all.

If you are home alone, and a caller scares you in any way by saying something like 'I know where you live and I'm coming to get you,' or 'I can see you right now,' hang up and call your neighbour and the police. You may not be in any real danger, but there's no point in waiting around to find out.

Safety in Lifts

Take these precautions:

If there aren't many people around, use the stairs. Running up and down stairs, where you have a chance of getting away from danger or knocking at a door for help, is much safer than being trapped in a lift.

Never get into a lift with anyone who makes you uneasy. Pretend you've forgotten something and say, 'Go ahead', then

use the stairs or wait for the next lift.

If you are in a block of flats, make sure the lift isn't headed for the basement. Basements can be dangerous.

If anyone makes you uneasy or bothers you, make the lift stop as soon as possible, get out, and run to the most populated area of the building. Call for help if you need to. Leave the building if you can.

Safety in School

It's important to stay alert even when you are at school:

Avoid deserted places in school. This is especially true if you are alone, out during a class period, or staying late.

If you see a suspicious-looking person hanging around the school, like a man who doesn't have any connection to the place, report him to a trusted teacher immediately. Child molesters can be attracted to schools. If he turns out to be legitimate, don't worry about feeling like a fool; you've been alert and

cautious and everyone should respect that.

If you know of anyone in the school molesting a pupil, report it. You aren't being a tell-tale, you are having the courage to bring to light a crime that many people are too afraid to face.

If you are bothered by anyone in the school, you have a right to stop him or her. This is true whether the person is a teacher, a friend, or even the Head. Being bothered can mean being touched or teased repeatedly against your will; receiving obscene phone calls; being threatened or bullied; or actually being sexually molested. A self-defence teacher told of how a fourteen-year-old girl handled persistent harassment by a fellow student:

A boy at school, who was somewhere between twelve and fourteen, liked this girl, but the only way he could show it was to pinch and poke her all the time. She told him twice to stop it, but he just said, 'Oh yeah, big tough you. What are you going to do about it?' When he did it the third time, she said, 'One more time and I'll hurt you.' He did it again, so she whirled around and did her self-defence kick into his knee. His knee was hurt - not permanently, but enough to stop him from bothering her. She became a heroine at school because this boy had been bothering a lot of people. Even the boy's parents were supportive because they didn't like the way their son treated girls.

Physical defence like this should be the last resort, but if someone is hurting you, you have the right to use enough physical force to stop it.

Safety While Babysitting

As harmless as babysitting seems, it does, unfortunately, make you somewhat vulnerable. You are alone in a house you may not be familiar with; you are working for people you may not know well; you have the responsibility of looking after the safety of young children; and you often have to go home late. Many of the rules listed under 'Safety at Home Alone' at the beginning of this chapter apply to babysitting, too, but here are some additions:

Meet your employers before you start. If you feel uneasy about either of them, don't take the job.

Work out your transport to and from the place before you start. A lift from your parents is the safest.

Let your parents know where the job is. Give them the phone number.

Always have the phone numbers of your parents, the police, the neighbours, and the children's doctor next to the phone. Try to have the number of wherever your employers will be as well.

Ask your employers not to arrange for deliveries or service calls when you are there alone. If they must, ask them to make sure to let you know whom to expect.

Never let anyone who rings the doorbell or calls know that you are the babysitter. That advertises that you are alone. If someone calls, say, 'I'm afraid Mr and Mrs X are busy right now. Can I take a message?'

Don't let the children answer the phone or door. They are easily tricked into letting people in or revealing that you are alone.

If you invite a boy over, don't let him think it's an invitation for sex. Remember, there's no one in the house you can rely on to interrupt or rescue you. Make it clear that your first priority is looking after the children. Always ask your employer if you can have a friend over.

Know the address of the house and directions to it by heart. That way, you can direct the police, fire station, or an ambulance if there's an emergency.

How To Handle Babysitting Emergencies

If you ever have to call an ambulance, the police or the fire station, give them the address first. People often forget to do this in their panic.

If someone forces his way into the house, or even if you hear suspicious noises, TAKE THE CHILDREN AND GET OUT OF THE HOUSE the back way, if you can. Go to a neighbour for help. If you can't get out, follow these steps:

◆ *Call the police if you have time, give them the address, and quickly say, 'Someone's breaking in.'*

◆ *Lock yourself into a room. If the children are awake and you can keep them quiet, bring them with you.*

◆ *Call the neighbours for help. They might be able to frighten the intruder away immediately.*

◆ *DON'T CONFRONT THE INTRUDER.*

◆ *DON'T LEAVE THE CHILDREN UNPROTECTED.*

If you get a frightening phone call, call your parents and a neighbour immediately. Sometimes people check to see if you are alone before breaking in.

If one of your employers tries to molest you in any way, report them immediately to your parents and never work for them again. Perhaps when the man is driving you home at the end of the evening, he tries to kiss you, puts his hand on your leg, or actually leaps on you and tries rape. Maybe the mother will try something on a boy she's hired. You are in a tricky position because you are younger, alone in their house or car, and intimidated by the fact that they are adults and your employers. If anything like this happens to you, fight back. Use the self-defence techniques described in the next chapter, and report the adult immediately. Don't let yourself be tricked or embarrassed into keeping the assault a secret; if you do, that adult will probably go on to assault other teenagers after you.

If your employer just makes you feel uncomfortable, perhaps by looking at you in a sexual way, by talking about sex a lot, by asking you too many personal questions, or by dropping hints that he wants to have 'an affair' with you, stop working for that person. Trust your instincts and remember that this behaviour can be the start of sexual assault, a way for him to test you out. If you pretend to ignore him and keep coming back to babysit, he may decide you'll be a compliant victim.

SELF-DEFENCE

Most successful self-defence tactics are non-physical. Self-defence means what it says: it's about defending yourself, not fighting. The first motto of self-defence is, The best self-defence is awareness and escape.

Self-defence methods increase your chances of stopping an assault, but they won't make you invulnerable. Regard the following tactics as a supplement to the self-protection you've already learned.

Have faith in your own strength and power. You are much stronger and faster than you probably realise. Most people never test themselves enough to find out what they can really do.

Think about what you'd do if you were assaulted. Try to select the methods that would suit you personally. If you have a strong voice, for example, yelling and shouting might suit you.

Whenever possible, try to find an alternative to physical

fighting. The less contact you have with an assailant, the safer you'll be.

ALWAYS TRUST YOUR INSTINCTS.

Non-Physical Self-Defence

You might be surprised to find out how much you and your body already know about non-physical self-defence. When we allow our survival instincts to work without the confusion of rationalising, guilt, or shame, those instincts can be extremely quick. Take the story of this twelve-year-old girl:

I was walking home from school carrying my flute in its case, when an older boy ran up and tried to grab it. I just screamed at the top of my lungs. He got so scared he started to shake, then he ran away.

And the story of this girl of thirteen:

I was in a phone box and a retarded boy came in and started hugging me. I don't think he meant any harm, but it scared me, so I slipped through his arms and ran home. My body just told me to do it.

And, finally, the story of this sixteen-year-old boy:

I was walking down the street minding my own business when I vaguely noticed five or six teenage boys walking in front of me. I didn't pay much attention because there were other people on the street, but suddenly they spread out over the pavement and when I walked through them, they started to hit and kick me. I pushed them aside, dashed ahead, and turned and looked at them and said, 'What's the matter with you guys? What are you doing? Are you crazy?' I was so astonished that they would do that, I spoke before I was even scared. They

*began glaring at me and coming at me, so I said, 'I'm
not going to fight with you' in a fed-up voice, and
turned around and walked away calmly. I was scared
by then, but I didn't show it.*

These three people, none of whom had been trained,
instinctively used the three basic strategies of non-physical
self-defence: the yell, the escape, and the talk.

The Yell

There's a big difference between the self-defence yell, which
some people call the Power Yell, and an ordinary scream. The
yell comes from deep in the stomach, not high in the throat,
and is like the yell that a karate or judo master uses before he
or she attacks. It's a battle cry, not a frightened screech. It's
the sound of anger and attack, not fear.

The yell is designed to do several things: break through that
moment when you might be frozen in panic or shock at
being attacked, startle the wits out of an attacker, make you
look strong and angry instead of weak and scared, and
attract attention.

You need to practise the yell. Try it now, into a pillow at home
or somewhere after you've warned the people within earshot.
Start by thinking of someone or some time that makes you
really angry, then yell whatever defiant word or sound comes
to mind: 'No!' 'Stop!' or whatever. If, when you practise it, it
makes you feel angry or upset, you're on the right track. If
you frighten yourself, even better.

When you use the yell is important - the sooner the better in
an attack. If you can yell the instant you sense danger, before
anyone has his hands on you, you are more likely to frighten
off the offender. If you are in a populated area, near people
who can hear you, the yell can bring you help. But if you are

in an isolated area, the man has already grabbed you, and you sense that your yell might make him angry or more violent, then don't do it. As always in self-defence, you'll have to use your own judgment of when to use a particular method.

Often the yell itself is enough to end an attack. Most molesters who go after people your age aren't expecting anything like a terrifying war cry. Look at the example of these two girls:

We were playing with a dog in the park, when a man came up to us and began saying obscene things we didn't like. We both instantly did the Power Yell we'd learned right at him. He ran off as fast as he could.

The Escape

Like the yell, escape works best when you can act the instant you recognise danger. Experts say there is an instant at the start of an attack when the offender is as uncertain and scared as you. That instant is usually the first moment of approach, when he steps into your path to block your way, for instance, or first says, 'Hey, what time is it?' As long as he doesn't have a gun pointed at you, this is the best moment to break away and run.

Escape is often the most successful when it's combined with the yell or with one of the physical forms of self-defence described later. The idea is to stun the offender into paralysis long enough to get away from him, the way this twelve-year-old girl did, according to the following newspaper story:

The girl was using a pay-phone in a shop one evening with a ten-year-old friend, a boy. Suddenly, she was grabbed by a man who tried to drag her into his car. Both kids did the Power Yell they had learnt in self-defence at school, and it stunned the man long enough to enable the girl to break out of his grip. She ran quickly to a nearby house. The police were called and told the direction in which the man was driving away. They caught him speeding and arrested him.

To escape successfully, you have to appraise your situation and look for an escape route. If there is a street behind you, for instance, and an isolated wood ahead of you, you'd want to run into the street, where there are people and houses. If you are being attacked by a date, you might have to plan your escape carefully and trick him into going somewhere you can get help. On the other hand, if you are trapped in a car with an offender, your escape might have to be as risky and sudden as opening the door and jumping out.

When the offender is someone in your household, running away might not be possible. The yell might work to stop the assault right at the moment, but talking and telling (see below and chapter eight) are needed to keep it from happening again.

Yelling and running the moment you sense danger are, combined, the most effective way of escaping assault. Even if you're not certain of the danger, don't be afraid to look silly; that's far better than taking a risk.

The Talk

Your voice can be one of your best weapons, especially when it is coupled with determination. Talking your way out of an attack can be as simple as an outright 'No, I won't' or as complex as a lengthy persuasion. If, for instance, someone tries to bribe or threaten you into having some kind of sex, an immediate and firm 'No' might be enough to dissuade him. Think about how good you are at being firm and direct when you talk to people. Do you look people in the eye? Do you speak loudly and clearly? Practise looking yourself in the eye in a mirror and saying 'No' loudly and firmly.

Another tactic you can use is the 'broken record' technique. That means saying something like 'No, I won't' over and over again to every question the offender asks.

For some offenders, even a strong, persistent 'No' doesn't work. It may, for example, only make them more angry and violent. If you see this happening, you will probably have to change your strategy from a simple firm refusal to something more complicated. That's what Celia found when she was walking home one night.

It was late, the street was deserted, and I was by myself, so I already felt rather nervous. Suddenly this weird-looking man drove by on a motorcycle, saw me, and swerved his bike around. He drove right up on the pavement in front of me and stopped. He looked pretty crazy and I knew I was in trouble. Then he began insulting me and saying things like 'What's a nice Jewish girl like you doing out so late?'

I could tell getting mad or huffy wasn't going to help, so I pretended I didn't understand what he meant. Instead, I said something like 'What a great bike you've got. Boy, am I glad you came along, because I was feeling scared.' He looked interested, so I kept going, and even though what I was saying sounded ridiculous to me, he began to look proud. I expect no one had ever said such nice things to him before. In the end, he let me go without touching me.

If Celia had been able to run somewhere safe, yell for help, or in any other way escape quickly, she would have taken less of a risk, but as it was she could tell those methods wouldn't work fast enough. So, she found words that defused her assailant's anger.

If an attacker responds to this sort of strategy with interest, or even if they just calm down, they may be the type who can be tricked. If so, keep talking along these lines while you work out a way to escape. Rapists are egomaniacs, so remember these two rules:

◆ *Keep the attention focused on him with words like 'What's made you so upset?'*

◆ *Keep yourself human in his eyes with phrases like 'This is scary for me, but maybe we can work it out.'*

Once you've manoeuvred him into a place or position that's safer for you, use one of these tactics:

◆ *Make a sudden physical self-defence move (see below) and run.*

◆ *Yell and escape.*

◆ *Trick or persuade him into letting you go.*

Say something like 'Just let me go to the bathroom.'

If your talking is making the attacker more angry, you'll be able to tell fast enough, so stop. The more angry he is, the more liable he is to hurt you. If you can't talk yourself out of an attack, can't trick the attacker, or can't escape, you may have to resort to the physical self-defence methods described below.

Verbal resistance often works best with people you know. If the offender is someone in your household or a boyfriend, the yell, a firm 'No,' and a threat to tell can effectively stop the abuse.

One girl who had been molested by her father every night for years finally put a stop to it by using a simple method she'd learned in a self-defence class: When he opened the door to her bedroom, she said loudly and cheerfully for the whole house to hear, 'What do you want, Dad?' He quietly left the room and never came to molest her again.

Physical Self-Defence

Several studies have been done over the years on whether physical resistance can help a woman escape a rape attack. The results have on the whole been encouraging. Women have escaped rape by yelling and running away, and many have also escaped by fighting back. Sometimes, though, struggling with a rapist can make him even more violent. Only you can decide whether to resist a sexual attack or not, and your decision has to depend on these questions:

Does the attacker have a weapon? Most attackers are not armed, but if you are threatened by someone who has a gun, resistance is not usually wise. If the assailant has a knife, there might be opportunities to get the knife away from him or to escape if he puts it down, but resistance without proper training in self-defence is difficult and risky.

How capable do you feel of resisting? A timid struggle or half-hearted attempt to hit the attacker won't help. You have to feel angry and powerful.

How dangerous is the immediate situation? If you are within earshot of people, or can run somewhere safe quickly, resistance could work. But if you are somewhere isolated, your chances of escape are much reduced.

Have you had training in self-defence? If you have, your chances of resisting successfully are stronger. See your phone book and the back of this book for places that teach self-defence.

There are only a few physical self-defence moves that can be taught safely in a book. Most need to be taught and practised in a class. In order to be able to use them in the midst of the panic you'll feel when attacked, you have to physically practise them so much that they become second nature. Also, remember that physical self-defence is serious and should never be used in a playful fight with friends. And don't forget that every physical move is enhanced if it can be accompanied by a blood-freezing Power Yell.

The Stand

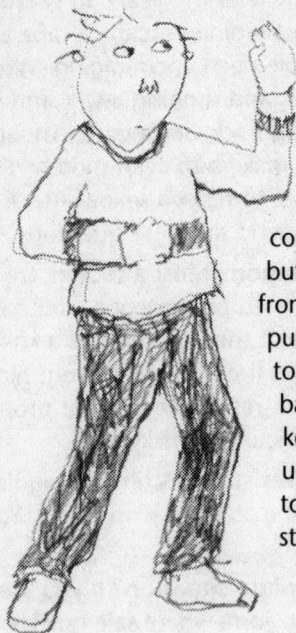

To give you power behind any kind of physical move, you need to be well balanced on your feet. Stand with your legs a shoulder-width apart, your hips balanced comfortably and your back straight but relaxed. Put one foot a little in front of the other so that you can't be pushed off balance easily. Ask a friend to push you until you find the right balance that keeps you steady. Now, keep your head up and your arms up and out, one in front of your face to protect it and one in front of your stomach.

The Kick

The kick is best to use because it keeps you at the farthest distance from the offender. Kick from the knee only, with a sharp forward action. Keep your toes up and snap your leg back immediately. Don't kick your whole leg and don't leave your leg sticking out after the kick. That makes it too easy for someone to grab it and tip you over. Think of the word snap when you kick. The kick works no matter how small you are because you can always reach an adult's knee or shin. Aim at the knee for most effect.

The Scrape

The scrape is best used if you are attacked from behind. First you do a sharp backward kick into the offender's kneecap, then you scrape your heel down his shin.

The Palm Heel

Hold your hand up and out, palm forward and fingers pointed
upwards. Keep your fingers slightly bent and close together
and your thumb next to your fingers so it doesn't get hurt.
Aim at the underside of the attacker's nose or chin, and thrust
hard and quick up into it with the heel of your hand. You can
hurt and stun someone long enough to escape from him in
this way.

The Elbow Hit

This can be used for attacks from behind and beside you.
Swivel around so that you are standing slightly sideways
compared to the assailant. Thrust your arm forward quickly,
fist clenched and facing upwards. Then bend your arm and
thrust quickly backwards with your elbow pointed into the
offender's groin or stomach. The harder you do it and the
straighter your elbow goes back, the more power you'll have.

The Instep Stamp

Lift your knee high and stamp down as hard as you can on the top of the offender's foot. You can use this whether he is facing you, behind you, or beside you.

The Spearhand Eye and Throat Jab

Hold your hand out straight and firm, wrist straight, fingers
  bent slightly at the tips.

Tuck your thumb into your palm so it's out of the way. This
  position is called the spearhand. It can be used to thrust hard
  and straight into an attacker's throat or eyes, depending on
  how high you can reach. If you hit him in the throat, it will
  cause temporary breathing difficulty - enough to give
  you some time to run. If you hit him in the eyes,
  you will hurt and daze him long enough to
  escape. You will not permanently blind him.

Breaking A Hold

If someone has his hands around your mouth from behind to prevent you from screaming, the best way to get out of it is to grab his little fingers and snap them backward. You can only do this if you have your hands free, of course, but it will hurt him enough to make him let go. Most people try to grab the assailant's arms, but that doesn't work.

If someone has his arm around your neck from behind, turn your head into his elbow. That way, you'll relieve the pressure from your throat so you can breathe.

Then try the backward kick, shin scrape, and instep stamp. A self-defence teacher told of how Michael, a boy of only eight, fought off two attackers with these methods. He had learned them in a few self-defence classes he'd taken with his mother.

One day when Michael was playing in his front yard, he was approached by a man drinking beer. The man had sweets and a BB gun. He said, 'Do you want some sweets?' Michael said, 'I don't talk to strangers,' as he'd been taught, and backed away. Then the man said, 'Do you want to look at my BB gun?' Michael again said, firmly, 'No.'

Suddenly, Michael saw a second man, also drinking beer. He stood behind Michael. The first man grabbed Michael, dragged him between two parked cars on the street, and started to molest him. Michael planted his feet to get his balance, kicked the man in the shin, scraped down his assailant's shin with his foot, stamped on his instep, did his yell, broke free, and ran to his neighbour's for help. The two men ran off in the other direction.

If an eight-year-old boy can fight off two men after only a few self-defence lessons, imagine what you can do!

8

GETTING HELP

If You Can't Escape

If you are attacked and can't escape no matter what, there are still ways you can protect yourself.

Take a few deep breaths. This will calm you down and help you recover from that first moment of panic. When you are calm, you can think clearly, and that helps you survive.

Examine the situation. Can you see an escape route? Can you persuade the attacker to put down his weapon by saying something like 'Look, I'll do what you say, you don't need that. It's just making me nervous.' Can you throw the weapon out of his reach if he does put it down?

Look at the attacker's face, if you can. Try to remember what he looks like, what he's wearing, how he talks, how he smells. This will help to catch and identify him later.

Keep thinking about how to escape. Even if you have to submit to the assault, you'll want to get away as fast as you can afterwards. And perhaps, during the assault, the attacker will leave his face vulnerable to an eye or nose jab.

There are two final methods of self-defence that can be used during an actual attack. The first is the eye-gouge – you put your hands on either side of the attacker's face, then suddenly push your thumbs into his eyes. This won't blind him, but it'll put him in enough pain to let you go. The second is the testicle squeeze - you take hold of his testicles and twist with as much force as you can. This could even knock him out. During an attack, when your survival instincts are working, you may be willing to do anything to save yourself.

Anyone who has been sexually abused in any way needs help. Abuse is an abnormal, terrifying event, and you should not be expected to cope with it on your own.

This chapter explains why you should never be too ashamed to tell, no matter what happens to you. And it explains why you deserve help, and how to get it.

The best way to help yourself recover from an assault is to turn to someone you love for sympathy. Many studies have found that people who can talk about the assault and who get sympathy and support from those close to them recover much better than people who keep the whole thing secret. So if you think you should keep your assault quiet so that you don't upset anyone or make them angry, think again. It would be much more upsetting for anyone who loves you, and for you yourself, to see you burdened by a terrible secret than to have it out in the open.

First of all, you must know that whatever has happened to you, it was not your fault. If you are afraid to seek help because you think you brought on the assault yourself, stop thinking like that now. You are not at fault, you are not a failure. You have a right to get all the help and sympathy you need.

Your Reactions to Sexual Assault

Straight after an attack of any kind, you are going to be in shock. Every person has his or her own way of reacting to shock, and lots of people react in different ways all in a row. One minute, for instance, you may feel calm and relieved, the next in such a panic you can't catch your breath. Many people find their emotions swinging wildly from one extreme to the next. A little later, you might find yourself almost as frightened by your reactions to the abuse as by the abuse itself. Suddenly you are full of terrors – scared of the dark, of men, of being alone, of certain places. You may have nightmares and trouble eating or sleeping for a while. 'Am I going crazy?' you may wonder. 'What is happening to me?'

What is happening is that you are having a normal reaction to an extremely abnormal event. Everyone has these reactions and you are not alone or weird to be feeling the way you do. People who've lived through other traumas, like fires and accidents, have the same kinds of reactions. You have been through a terrible experience and you will need time to get over it. As Karen, the girl who was raped in the park, said:

The counsellor I went to told me, 'One day, this will be a thing that happened to you and not a major tragedy.' I thought, 'How insensitive. She doesn't understand.' But I realised today that it's been three years and now it is just a thing that happened. As my mother put it, I had to go through a period of mourning.

It may take as long as three years before the assault is 'just something that happened,' but it probably won't take that long for you to be able to get back to a normal, happy state of being. You won't forget the assault – no one can – but you will find a way of living without letting it dominate your life. Most people take between three months and a year to get over the fears and depression an assault causes. That may seem like a long time, but you will get through it. Almost everybody does.

Who To Tell About Incest

If you are being sexually assaulted by a member of your family, you have two major tasks to accomplish: to stop the assaults, and to recover from them. Most likely you will need to get someone else's help. Here are the possibilities to consider.

Can you tell a sister or brother? Sometimes the offender is molesting all the children in the family and they are keeping it secret from each other. If your sister, for example, has been molested too, it might be easier for both of you to seek help together than for either of you to do it alone.

Can you tell your mother (or, if she is the offender, your father)? You may have avoided telling your mother for various reasons, but think carefully about whether you are being fair to her. Are you sure that her fear of facing the truth would be stronger than her desire to protect you?

It is true that the news will be a shock to your mother. If she loves your father, stepfather, whoever he is, she's going to be deeply shocked when she finds out what he's been doing to you. She might get angry at you at first. She might not want to believe you because she can't face the truth. She's going to feel betrayed by him, maybe disgusted by him. And she's going to be shattered at what's happened to her family. On top of all this, she's going to have to decide whether to tell the police and whether to leave him. For these reasons, you

might want to turn to someone other than your mother at first. Remember, though, that she's going to have to know in the end, and that she can end up being more of a help and comfort to you than anyone else in the world.

Which other adults could you tell first? If you think your mother would be too upset, wouldn't believe you, or would get angry with you, another adult who does believe you can help to calm her down and comfort both of you. Could you tell a friend's mother, perhaps? A teacher or a doctor? Another relative, like an aunt? That person, with your permission, could either tell your mother or help you decide what to do next. This was the case for Betsy...

Whenever Betsy was alone with her grandfather, he began to talk about the sexual acts he wanted to do with her. He also tried to bribe her to kiss and hug him. She became more and more scared, and finally told a self-defence teacher at school about it. Betsy said, 'I love my grandfather and my family does too, so I can't tell them.'

The teacher asked Betsy if she could call her mother so that all three of them could talk about it. Betsy agreed, and her mother was very understanding and concerned. She believed Betsy, listened carefully to everything she said, and then decided to tell the grandfather to stop. She also decided that Betsy would no longer be left alone with him.

Can you tell a friend? If you have a close friend whom you trust, you might find it easier to go to an adult with their help. This happened to Jennifer when she finally decided to tell a self-defence teacher about her abuse. The teacher said:

Jennifer came to get help because her father had been sexually abusing her for years. With her came her best friend, Luisa, who knew all about the abuse. As Jennifer told her story, there were times when she cried so hard she couldn't speak. Each time, Luisa picked up the story, explaining what had happened and encouraging Jennifer to go on. With the help of her friend, Jennifer was able to do something she might not have been able to do alone.

If a friend of yours is being abused, you can be like Luisa and help her or him tell an adult.

Can you call a professional counsellor for help? There is a list of places to call at the back of this book, but first you'll probably have several important questions you'll want answered.

If I tell a professional counsellor, or any adult for that matter, will the police, or my family, have to know?

Most centres that deal with sexual assault keep all their cases entirely confidential. They won't tell anyone against your will, even your parents. If you want to make doubly sure, call the centre and ask about their policy before you give them your name or story. You can always refuse to give your name or use a fake one.

If I tell and the police find out, will my father (or whoever the offender is) go to prison?

Not necessarily. The police will put your family in contact with either a social services department or a counselling service such as the Victim Support Scheme, who will then talk to your family, find out what the problem is, and look at all the possible situations that can keep the family together and avoid arrest, if that's what you want. If you and your family don't want the offender to go to prison, it's unlikely that he will, for your cooperation will be needed to prove him guilty.

If I tell and the authorities find out, will I be taken away from my family?

It depends on your own safety and wishes. If you are removed, you are usually put in an institution or a foster home until you can go back home.

If I tell, will my family hate me?

Not if you find a counsellor to explain to your family what is happening and why they should be on your side. Some offenders hate what they are doing and are glad to get some help with stopping it. At first your family probably will be upset, but in the end they will most likely be grateful.

What To Do After A Sexual Assault

When you've been molested or sexually assaulted, your first priority is your own safety. This is the order of action you should take:

Go somewhere safe. If you were attacked outside, get away from the attacker and the place it happened as soon as possible. Go to a shop, the police, a hospital, a friend's house, your home - whichever is nearest and safest. If you were attacked at home, you might want to get out. At the same time, you shouldn't be alone and vulnerable on the streets. So, as soon as you can, get to a phone and call for someone to come and collect you.

Decide whom to call. Your mother? A friend? The police? An ambulance? Most teenagers either call their parents immediately or keep the assault a secret from everyone, not seeking help at all. You should seek help right away because you are going to feel terrified. You need and deserve comfort. If you are certain your family couldn't handle the news, or that you couldn't stand their reactions to it, you may want to turn to a counselling centre instead, at least for the time being.

You'll probably want to have someone with you right after the assault to see you through those first terrible hours when you are so shaken and scared. No one likes to be alone after an assault. On the other hand, you may, like the fifteen-year-old daughter of this woman, want to cope with almost everything yourself:

When my daughter was raped, she stayed really calm about it. She told me, but she insisted on going to the hospital and telling the police on her own. She was so grown-up and capable about it, I was amazed.

After a sexual assault, you need to take back control over your life as soon as possible. For some people, that means making their own decisions and coping with everything on their own. If you are able to do that, it can help you to heal. But don't deny yourself help just to look heroic.

Telling the police. If you tell the police immediately, and particularly if you tell them before you have washed or changed your clothes, the advantage is that they'll be able to gather evidence of the assault straight away, which will help them catch and prosecute the man who did it. If you cannot face the police immediately, you can still tell them later. This does make their job more difficult, but it's better to report assault late than not at all.

The police have child protection teams in many areas who are trained to deal with young victims of sexual assault. They have special offices, which contain a few quiet rooms where you can be medically examined, have a thorough wash in a fully equipped bathroom, and sit in comfort and privacy while being interviewed.

The police have close contacts with people who are specially trained in helping people after an attack. These people will give you help to recover from your ordeal and will prepare you if the case goes to court. They will also sit with you while you talk to the police.

After you have had a medical examination, the police will ask you to tell them exactly what happened, and the interview will probably be recorded on a video film. They'll want to find out who abused you, what he (or she) looked like, what they wore, what they smelled like, whether you knew them before, how you met them, how they approached you – every detail. The police will also need to know every detail of what the assailant did to you -no matter how embarrassing. They may also take pictures of you, especially if you are bruised, dishevelled or otherwise hurt.

Some of the questions the police ask may seem unnecessary, even insulting, like 'Have you had sex with this man before?' but they do need to check the exact circumstances and if the case goes to court you will have to be prepared for similar questions. No one can promise that going to the police is pleasant. But, reporting an assault is the only way the assailant is going to be caught, and the only way the assailant is going to be stopped from doing it to someone else.

The Medical Examination. The police will ask you to agree to be examined by a specially-trained doctor. Normally you will be able to have a woman doctor if you want one, and a friend, parent or counsellor can stay with you or wait outside if you'd rather. This examination will help the doctor to make sure that you get any medical help you need as a result of the attack. It will also allow the doctor to gather evidence that will make convicting the rapist easier if he is caught.

As well as giving you an internal examination, the doctor will also look your body over for other signs of assault, like bruises and scratches. He or she may also want to take small samples from parts of your body that will be collected for evidence.

Within a few days of the assault, you will also have to have tests for sexually transmitted diseases. If you are afraid of getting pregnant from the rape, a hospital can test you for that, too, and help you with the consequences. Pregnancy from rape is a risk, but only a small one.

Even if you decide not to go to the police after an assault, you can go to the emergency department of a hospital for a medical examination instead. It is very important that you have medical attention after an attack.

Coping With Parents

You need the help and support of your parents, for they can encourage your recovery more than anyone else. They can help you feel good about yourself again, make you feel loved and protected again, and help you get back your faith in the good side of life. If you need to tell them with the help of another friend, a rape counsellor, or a teacher, do. In the end, it will be worth it.

Here are some of the main reasons you may not want to tell your parents, and what to do about them:

I'm afraid they'll get angry at me, blame me, or punish me for getting assaulted. Try talking to them with the help of an adult friend, teacher, or counsellor who's on your side. If this isn't enough, tell them that if they want to help you get better, they should talk to a rape crisis counsellor. They need to understand that what happened to you wasn't your fault.

I'm too embarrassed to discuss anything as intimate as sexual assault with them. Try to remember that sexual assault is primarily a crime of violence, not sex; what's important is that you were hurt and frightened.

I'm just getting my own privacy and independence apart from my parents; I don't want to undo that by involving them in this assault. It is especially traumatic to be assaulted when you are just experimenting with a little freedom. It can make you feel as if you're being punished for trying to grow up. But even though the assault will make you scared for a while, even though it makes it more difficult to trust people, it won't stop you from becoming independent. If, for now, you need to retreat into the nest of your family again - that's fine. Even adults usually want to be coddled and comforted when something bad happens, and families are supposed to give us comfort and support. Don't give up on your independence. Don't let your excitement about the world and all its possibilities get spoiled by your assault. But for now, do let yourself be protected if that's what you need. You have a whole life of independence before you, and although you'll be feeling more timid for a while, the assault won't stop you from growing up strong.

I don't want to upset and hurt my parents. This is a noble sentiment, but not appropriate right now. It would hurt most parents a lot more to see you upset but not know what's wrong, or to find out years later what happened and know they'd never had the chance to help you, than to hear the truth now.

I don't want them to find out what I was doing when the assault happened. If you were doing something you weren't supposed to when you were assaulted, like drinking, seeing someone your parents don't like, or even buying drugs, you may be afraid your parents will blame you or punish you. You or a counsellor should remind them that breaking rules is not the same as inviting an assault. Ask yourself whether your prediction of their attitude is accurate. Would your parents really be angry about what you were doing, or just concerned about whether you are all right?

I'm afraid to tell because my assailant threatened to kill me if I do. A lot of rapists and molesters use threats and lies to keep their victims quiet. Whatever the lie, try not to believe it. Remember, the molester is a criminal and he's trying to protect himself from getting caught. And if he's using threats, ask yourself how likely it really is that he could carry them out. Does he really know where you live and who you are? Would he really risk exposing himself by seeking revenge on you? If you think there is a real danger, talk to the police or a help agency about what to do to protect yourself and your family until the offender is arrested.

Once your parents do know about your assault, there will still be problems. Even the most understanding of parents will probably make mistakes. They may try to overprotect you. If you see this happening, remind yourself of how bad they feel about your assault. Explain that you understand this, but that the assault has not made you or your needs different. You need to grow up and you need to be independent. With all you've learned about protecting yourself, you'll be able to do that more safely.

Occasionally, your parents, especially your father, may react with such horror and embarrassment that they withdraw from you. Or members of your family might react by wanting to hunt the offender down.

If any of these problems become more than you can cope with, which is not unusual, you and your family should go to a help organisation. The counsellors are familiar with these kinds of troubles and know how to help you talk to each other and sort them out.

Coping With Friends

Choosing which friends to tell, if any, is extremely difficult. A lot of your friends won't know much about sexual assault – some may not even know what it is. The whole subject will probably embarrass them, and maybe even make them shy away from you. It's important, therefore, to think carefully about whom to tell.

If you decide not to tell anyone, you will again be faced with a very lonely time. Carrying around a secret like that makes you feel different from everyone else and shut off from them. So, look over your friends. Would any of them be sympathetic? Can you trust any of them not to go blabbing the news all over school?

If you do decide to tell a friend, don't be surprised if they are embarrassed for a while, or if they make insensitive remarks like 'Why didn't you just run away?' It's hard for anyone to say the right thing all the time, especially about something as shocking and frightening as sexual assault.

Everyone who's been assaulted is afraid they'll be seen as strange and different. Fears like these can, unfortunately, be justified because most people understand so little about sexual assault and are insensitive to it. Some teenagers refuse to go back to their old school after an assault because everyone knows about it. If you do go back, however, and you find that friends are making jokes at your expense or keeping away from you out of embarrassment, get help.

Tell a teacher or your parents so that those pupils can be taken aside and educated about sexual assault. Don't keep quiet, for you have suffered enough.

The best way to cope with friends after an assault is to tell only one or two who are very close to you and whom you trust. Dealing with school will be much easier if everyone doesn't know.

Coping With Your Boyfriend

If you are a girl and have a steady boyfriend, you'll probably want him to know about your abuse. If your relationship is close, the secret will be too much to keep to yourself. And the assault will alter your feelings about sex, too, for a while.

If he reacts by getting furious at the attacker, tell him his fury isn't comforting you, it's just making you scared.

Suggest that he call a counselling service to answer any questions he might have. A counsellor can explain to your boyfriend that if he can prove that he respects and likes you as much as ever, and can show you that he doesn't blame you in any way, he can help you recover.

Coping For Boys

If you are a boy, your problems after a sexual assault are unique. You have been the victim of a crime some people don't even know exists, and you may rightly fear that people will see you as some kind of freak as a result. You may have questions like these:

Why did it happen to me instead of someone else? Do I look funny, weak, or helpless? You were not picked on because of your looks or what you're like. You were picked on because you were there. Don't blame yourself for the assailant's problems.

Did the assault happen because I'm gay without knowing it? No. Whether you are gay or not has nothing to do with the assault. Often an attacker will say, 'You're just a faggot,' but he's only trying to justify what he's doing. He probably says that to every male he assaults. An assault is no reflection of your sexuality.

Will the assault turn me gay? No. A sexual assault cannot change a person's sexuality, even if it's committed by a man on a man. The most it will do is put you off making love or being touched by anyone, male or female, until you are over the shock. Don't worry - that is the usual reaction. It will pass.

Won't everyone think I'm gay if they find out? There is a danger that people will think so because few understand that sexual assault is more about violence than sex. A male who molests another male is doing it to conquer and humiliate, not out of desire. Choose whom to tell very carefully.

I am gay and that's why this happened. I'm being punished. Like many gay teens and adults, you might blame your sexuality for the assault. Because you may already feel like an outsider, like someone society doesn't approve of, it's easy to think that you were assaulted as some kind of punishment. 'This shows how much society hates me', is one way people look at it. 'This is what I get for living an 'abnormal' life-style', is another. A lot of gays and lesbians even feel deep down that they somehow deserved the assault because of their life-style, that they brought it on by being 'different'. All victims of crime tend to blame themselves at times and it never makes sense. Much of the time, assailants neither know nor care about your sexual preferences; you are just an available victim to them. Don't take on a criminal's problems as your own. You are innocent of wrongdoing and you deserve as much sympathy and help as anyone who is ever assaulted.

If you are gay and have been assaulted, however, you should be careful in selecting people to turn to for help. You won't be helped much by someone who tends to blame you or is full of prejudice. If you decide to use a counselling service and find your counsellor unsympathetic, you should ask for someone else.

Why couldn't I defend myself? Strong, grown-up, athletic men get assaulted, too. Muscles and macho are no match for a gun, a knife, a group of men, or even just being taken by surprise.

How can I tell a friend or girlfriend about this? You may worry that your friends will look down on you or see you as a freak if they find out, and that your girlfriend will see you as unmasculine or polluted by the assault. It's important to explain to them all you've learned here about assaults on males. Tell them it happens a lot, that it's an act of violence, not lust, and that you were victimized out of pure bad luck, not because of what you did or how you look. Tell them that 8 per cent of males are sexually abused at some point during their childhood.

Am I ever going to be able to feel sexual again after this? Yes, you are. But you may not be ready for a while. You need to get your self-respect back, and you need to be able to feel confident enough to relax. No one can feel sexual when they are scared, upset, and shocked.

I was assaulted by a woman. Am I wrong to feel upset? No. A woman who molests a boy is after power and revenge, just like a man. She's using unfair advantages of authority and age to use your body and maybe hurt you, too. Sex should always be a matter of choice and love. You have a right to be angry and hurt.

Boys and men tend to shy away from counsellors, because they are ashamed or they think counselling centres are only for women and girls. But counsellors have seen plenty of boys and men. There are even centres that are devoted exclusively to helping male victims. (See chapter nine.) Don't deny yourself the comfort, assurance, and advice you need.

Coping With Sex

If you're like anyone else who's been seriously assaulted, girl or boy, man or woman, you're wondering if you'll ever like sex again. Studies have found that assaulted adults and teenagers are able to enjoy making love again, but that it takes time. A sexual assault puts almost everyone off sex at first. You are not alone.

You may not want to be touched by anyone at all for a while. You may not even like your mother patting you, let alone anyone kissing you. So if your boyfriend or girlfriend pressurises you to make love in some way and you aren't ready, don't. You need to heal before you can feel sexual again. Don't ever make yourself do anything sexual you don't want to – it'll feel like being assaulted all over again.

If you don't have a steady boyfriend or girlfriend, you may not feel ready to start going out with anyone for a while. You'll find it hard to trust people you don't know or to be alone with a new date. Again, don't push yourself. Wait until you feel more secure, then maybe only go out with groups of friends for a while. It may take a month, it may take a year, but you will get back to normal.

If you were a virgin when you were assaulted, or you'd had very little sexual experience, you might be afraid that the experience will put you off sex for life. This doesn't have to be so. Karen, who has been quoted before, was a virgin when she was raped, yet listen to what she says about it now:

When I started having real sex for the first time with my boyfriend a year after the rape, I discovered that the two experiences were so different I didn't even have to compare. The rape was horrible, but the lovemaking was beautiful.

To her, quite rightly, sex was an expression of love while the rape had been an act of violence. She came to think of the rape as an accident – nothing to do with her love life. If you can look at your assault that way too, you'll go a long way towards getting over it.

SOURCES OF SAFETY

Safety Numbers

This section contains names, addresses and telephone numbers of help organisations, listed alphabetically, for victims of sexual and other types of abuse.

CHILDLINE

A free national telephone helpline for children and teenagers in trouble or danger. It is staffed by a team of experienced male and female counsellors who will listen and support any child with any problem.

◆ *Ring 0800-1111*

Or write to Childline, Freepost 1111, London N1 OBR

CHILDREN FIRST

Provides information about services available in Scotland.

◆ *Ring 0131-337-8539*

(Monday-Friday 9am-5pm)

Or write to Children First, Melville House,
41 Polworth Terrace, Edinburgh EH11 1NU

CHILDREN'S LEGAL CENTRE

Provides information on a wide range of children's issues, as well as a free and confidential legal advice line.

◆ *Ring 01206-873820*

(Monday-Friday 2pm-5pm,
and also Wednesday 10am-12pm)

Or write to Children's Legal Centre, University of Essex,
Wivenhoe Park, Colchester, Essex CO4 3SQ

CITIZENS ADVICE BUREAUX

Trained counsellors can give you details of local services available and help identify which is most relevant to your needs. Find your local branch in your telephone directory under 'Citizens'.

INCEST CRISIS LINE

A telephone counselling service for anyone involved in incest. It is run by volunteers, both men and women who have been victims of sexual abuse.

◆ *Ring 01752-666777*

NCH ACTION FOR CHILDREN

Provides a network of centres giving support to children who have been sexually abused and their families.

◆ *Ring 0171-226-2033*

*Or write to NCH Action for Children,
85 Highbury Park, London N5 1UD.*

NSPCC National Society for Prevention of Cruelty to Children. A nationwide organisation which deals with all aspects of child abuse. It provides a 24-hour service for children, parents and professional workers. Your local office will be listed under NSPCC in your telephone directory. There is a free helpline (24 hours).

◆ *Ring 0800-800-500 (free helpline)*

◆ *or 0171-825-2500 (for the central office)*

Or write to NSPCC, 42 Curtain Road, London EC2A 3NH

POLICE In an emergency dial 999. The police will respond 24 hours a day to calls anywhere in the UK.

RAPE CRISIS CENTRES A confidential counselling service run by women, for women and girls who have been sexually assaulted or raped. There is a national network of centres.

◆ *Ring 0171-837-1600 (6pm-10pm weekdays, 10am-10pm weekends)*

or look in your telephone directory under 'Rape Crisis Centre' for the number of your local centre.

SAMARITANS

A 24-hour counselling service for anyone depressed, lonely or suicidal. It is nationwide and your local branch can be found under 'Samaritans' in your telephone directory.

SOCIAL SERVICES DEPARTMENT

This is listed in your telephone directory under the town or city in which you live. There are usually emergency numbers you can use out of office hours.

SURVIVORS

A helpline offering couselling and support to male victims of sexual abuse.

◆ *Ring 0171-833-3737*

Or write to Survivors, PO Box 2470, London W2 1NW

VICTIM SUPPORT SCHEME

A nationwide group of nearly 400 schemes offering support and practical help to victims of violence and crime.

◆ *Ring 0171-735-9166*

Or write to Cranmer House, 39 Brixton Road, London SW9 6DZ

YOUTH ACCESS

This offers information about the types of youth counselling available all over the country.

◆ *Ring 01509-210420*

Or write to 13-25 Ashby House, 62A Ashby Road, Loughborough LE11 3AE

Organisations for Parents and Teachers

KIDSCAPE

An organisation that works with parents, teachers, police, youth leaders and children to prevent all types of assault and bullying. For further information about KIDSCAPE, and free leaflets, send a stamped addressed envelope to:

KIDSCAPE, 152 Buckingham Palace Road, London SW1W 9TR

◆ *Or ring 0171-730-3300*

PARENTS ANONYMOUS

A helpline for parents who are under stress or have problems with their children.

◆ *Ring 0171-263-8918 (7pm-12am)*

Self-Defence

Details of self-defence classes can usually be found at your local library, police station, Citizens Advice Bureau or Council Recreation Department.

NOTE FOR PARENTS

The idea of a sexual assault, or rape, or kidnapping, happening to our sons or daughters is so terrifying that often we can't bear to think about it. Instead, we vow to keep an eye on our children every minute and we say to ourselves, 'That won't happen to my child.'

Refusing to face the problem will not, of course, help to protect anyone. In fact, assailants rely on the ignorance of children and teenagers to turn them into victims. As parents, we only have one choice: we have to protect our children as much as we can and, perhaps more important, teach them to protect themselves.

Most assailants of children know their victims and, to entrap them, they rely less on violence than on the children's ignorance about sexual abuse. That means that a child or teenager who knows what sexual abuse is, and knows how to escape the danger before anything happens, has an excellent chance of avoiding being abused. Young teenagers are still very dependent on their parents' opinions, even if they outwardly reject them, and if they know you approve of and encourage their attempts to learn about sex, its pleasures and its dangers, they will feel much stronger. If you also support their attempts to learn self-protection - in the street, with people, on dates, at home - and actual self-defence, they will be doubly strong.

How To Help Your Teenager To Be Safer

Discuss family rules openly. Make the rules clear and explain that your primary concern is for your teenager's safety. Tell your teenager to ring you any time help is needed, with no fear of punishment. Promise that you will come to the rescue with no questions asked, no anger, and no punishment, even if rules have been broken. Later, after all the fear has died down, you are certainly entitled to bring up the subject and express your concern about it. But keep your promises and remember that this kind of arrangement can be one of the most important safety valves your child can have.

Tell your child that you never want him or her to feel unable to tell you about a frightening event for fear of punishment. Their trust in you should be more important than rules. Explain too that you'd rather be told about something like a sexual assault than be kept in the dark because your child doesn't want to upset you.

Encourage your son or daughter to take a self-defence class. (See 'Sources of Safety'.)

If Your Child Is Assaulted

The assault of your child is without doubt one of the most shattering things that can happen to you. There is the agony of seeing someone young and innocent suffer from such a sordid crime. There is the terror that your child has been damaged for life. There is the terrible guilt at having failed to protect your child. There is the wish that the assault had happened to you instead. Above all, there is the pain of seeing someone you love so much hurt so badly. The entire family will suffer, as well as the victim. You are what psychologists call 'secondary victims'.

The fact that you are so shattered by the assault of your child makes it more difficult to give the support he or she needs. Yet your support is essential. In order to avoid making mistakes that will increase your child's suffering, remember these facts:

Sexual assault is never the victim's fault. If your son or daughter was taking a risk, breaking a rule, or being careless, he or she was being a normal adolescent, not inviting an assault. Your child was horribly unlucky and it isn't fair to blame him or her for it.

Despite myths to the contrary, very few children make up stories about being sexually assaulted. Often they are too ignorant to even know that such things happen. You may want to disbelieve your child out of a need to deny the horror of it, but doing so will only make your child feel worse.

Sexual assault is a terrible tragedy, but young people are resilient. With your support and understanding, your child has more chance of recovering than many an adult.

How To Help Your Child Recover

Right after the assault, follow these steps:

◆ *Assure your child that you love, respect and believe him or her.*

◆ *Tell your teenager that you know the assault wasn't his or her fault. Without such assurance children are prone to blame themselves.*

◆ *Ask if he or she wants to go to the hospital, a Rape Crisis Centre, and the police right after the assault or later.* It's important that you offer to be there, but let your child make the decision about whether he or she would rather go alone. Because sexual assault robs the victim of all sense of control and self respect, it's very important to let your child make decisions right away.

◆ *After the initial crisis:*

Remember that you will need sympathy, too. Let yourself talk to someone else about the assault and your feelings, a counsellor if need be. But around your child, concentrate on his or her needs.

Suggest contacting a counselling service. Don't force your child to do it, but if you think it's needed as time goes on, gently suggest it again. Offer to participate in the sessions but don't insist.

Don't change the rules about when and where your child can go out now. A teenager in particular needs to know that the assault hasn't infringed on his or her attempts to grow up.

Don't keep treating your child as special or fragile. Like any victims of assault, teenagers need to feel that life can be normal again, that they aren't different, and that they aren't responsible for disrupting their family's life.

On the other hand, don't force your child to get back to

normal immediately. Your child may need a few days out of school, or a light on at night, or not to be left alone. Be sensitive to these needs.

Expect your child to go through a difficult period. Normal reactions to sexual assault include insomnia, nightmares, phobias, and reluctance to see friends. These reactions might start immediately after the assault, but they might not come up until several days or weeks later. The victim is also likely to go through a phase of denying that the assault is traumatic. Often the trauma comes out in seemingly unrelated ways, like recurrent headaches or stomach troubles or other physical ills. If your child is having symptoms like these and is denying the assault, get help from a doctor and suggest counselling.

Reassure your teenager that reactions like those described above are normal and happen to everyone after a sexual assault. Your child may fear that he or she is going crazy.

Keep telling your child that you love and respect him or her. Children often feel extremely unlovable after a sexual assault. They need to know they are still attractive and nice. They also need to feel proud of having survived such an ordeal.

Don't drop the subject of the assault forever. If you do, it'll become a forbidden subject in the family, which will make it impossible for your teenager to ask questions about it or talk about it when he or she needs to.

Expect family tensions to result from this trauma. There will be fights and explosions. You and your spouse might blame each other for the assault. Your other children may get jealous of the attention the victim is getting, or feel guilty that it didn't happen to them. If things get out of hand, consider family counselling through a help organisation.

If your son or daughter is miserable at school, discuss what can be done about it. Ask your teenager if you can discuss the problem with the teachers. It may even be necessary to change schools.

How To Recognise That Your Child Has Been Assaulted

Here are some symptoms that might indicate a sexual assault. If you see any of them, ask your child gently if he or she has been hurt by someone, is scared about something, or is upset. Make sure you say, 'I won't be angry because I know it's not your fault, but I want to know so I can help.'

Any extremely sudden change of behaviour. This can include not going out any more, not coming home, not eating, or eating too much.

Sudden depression, quietness, or explosions of anger.

Rapid gain or loss of weight.

Sudden uncharacteristic obsessions with sex, or, in a boy, with homosexuality.

Abrupt display of delinquent behaviour. This includes taking drugs, staying out late, picking fights, skiving off school, failing classes – anything that reflects a sudden loss of self-esteem or tendency toward self-punishment.

Sudden aversion to a certain person or place.

Dramatic reaction of fear or distress at a violent or sexual scene in a movie.

Nightmares, crying spells, insomnia.

Dressing differently, such as wearing many layers of clothes. Children who've been sexually assaulted often try to cover up their bodies as if to hide – this is not the same as trying to look fashionable.

Washing obsessively or not at all.

Deliberately hurting him – or herself.

Of course, these symptoms don't necessarily mean your child has been sexually assaulted, but they certainly mean something is wrong.

Assault By A Family Member

If your son or daughter has been sexually assaulted, be prepared for the possibility that the assailant is someone in your family. It will be very difficult for your child to tell you this, so as painful as it is for you to hear, you must be as supportive as you can. Believing your child and protecting him or her will, in the long run, help the whole family, the offender included. Here are some suggestions to help you handle this tragic event:

Protect your son or daughter – and other children – from further assaults. If you can find a way of doing this without sending them away from home, so much the better. Stay with them if you can. Leave with them if you must. Don't leave any of your children alone with the offender. Arrange for a friend or relative to stay with them if you must go to work.

Let your child go to school and have as normal a life as possible, as long as it doesn't put him or her in danger. Your child needs to feel that life can go on normally.

Confront the offender. If you can't do it on your own, for fear of violence or any other reason, think of whose help you can enlist. Other family members? Friends? A therapist?

Seek help. See 'Sources of Safety'.

Don't try to cope with everything on your own. Discovering that someone you love is a child molester is deeply shattering. You deserve all the comfort and counselling you can get.

Call the police. If the offender is a danger to any of your children or you, call the police. An arrest or even a warning will stop the abuse, at least temporarily. Many families don't want to take legal action against the offender. Perhaps the offence seems too mild; perhaps you love the offender too much. You may be tempted to believe this was an aberration and will never happen again, but be warned – child molesters rarely do it only once. Don't forget your child, out of the wish to protect the offender or to deny that this horrible thing happened. Help your child get free from the assaults and help the offender stop committing them if you can, but above all don't let things continue as they are. If you do, your son or daughter will be scarred for life.

If you can inform yourself about the realities of sexual assault – what it is, who commits it, how it affects people – you can do a great deal to help your child be safer. And that is giving your child strength that will last a lifetime.